Tocqueville and the Problem of Democracy

D0897826

TOCQUEVILLE

and the Problem of Democracy

———————

MARVIN ZETTERBAUM

1967
Stanford University Press
Stanford, California

Stanford University Press
Stanford, California
© 1967 by the Board of Trustees of the
Leland Stanford Junior University
Printed in the United States of America
L.C. 67-13664

To Evelyn

Preface

A century and a quarter ago Alexis de Tocqueville broke in on the intellectual world with the astonishing pronouncement that democracy and democratic governments were inevitable, that they were soon to be the rule everywhere. Indeed, for a time this pronouncement seemed clearly correct: for the civilized countries democracy was right around the corner, while for their less fortunate cousins the way would be only a bit longer and more arduous. Oddly enough, however, at the close of the nineteenth century, when the prospects of the democratic revolution were seemingly at their peak, the man who had alerted the West to the inevitability of that revolution was forgotten, or at least unread. This was unfortunate, for Tocqueville could have been counted on to remind his readers that hosannas were premature, that much hard work remained in order (in Pierson's phrase) to "make *démocratie* safe for the world."

Tocqueville's "inevitability thesis" has prevented many readers from coming to terms with his central concern, the problem of democracy, by drawing their attention to two other concerns: whether democracy was or was not inevitable, and whether the concept of historical inevitability was valid. Today, when the triumph of democracy seems anything but inevitable, and the belief in historical inevitability itself is on the wane, it seems especially appropriate to place Tocqueville's inevitability thesis in its proper perspective, the perspective he intended. As I endeavor to show in Chapter i of this book, the inevitability thesis was simply a convenient means to focus men's attention on what Tocqueville really cared about: the task of perfecting democracy, of reconciling the demands of justice with those of excellence. The succeeding chapters explore the dimensions of this task and the principal instrument by which he sought to achieve it: the doctrine of self-interest rightly understood. I attempt to show that although Tocqueville ultimately failed in his enterprise, his failure has significance for us in disclosing the permanent components of any genuine solution to the problem of democracy.

A portion of the first chapter appeared originally as "Tocqueville: Neutrality and the Use of History," in the *American Political Science Review* of September 1964, and I wish to thank the editor of that journal for permission to reprint this material here. My thanks also go to Rand McNally and Co., publishers of the *History of Political Philosophy*, edited by Leo Strauss and Joseph Cropsey, for permission to borrow extensively from my chapter on Tocqueville in that volume. For permission to quote from Phillips Bradley's edition of *Democracy in America* I am grateful to Alfred A. Knopf, Inc. I am grateful also for financial assistance from the University of California and the Relm Foundation.

More years ago than I like to recall, Allan Bloom first suggested that I turn to a study of Alexis de Tocqueville, and he has encouraged me in this enterprise ever since. For specific suggestions during the course of my inquiry I am indebted to Martin Diamond, Morton Frisch, Harry Jaffa, Richard Stevens, Herbert Storing, and Bernate Unger. Joseph Cropsey and Ralph Lerner have each gone over the manuscript with meticulous care and gentlemanly consideration; it is a scarcely sufficient sign of my gratitude to absolve them here from any responsibility for my errors of fact or judgment. My indebtedness to those Tocqueville scholars who have labored before me is evident in the pages that follow. To Leo Strauss I owe a debt that far transcends this immediate study. Finally, my wife, to whom this volume is dedicated, provided assistance at every stage of the research and writing; more than this, she supplied the support and the conviction that the deed would be done.

M. Z.

Davis, California
September 1966

Contents

Tocqueville and the Problem of Democracy

. . . as though it would do for them to be like passengers on shipboard, brought thither each for his own ends and by his own choice, uniting to act for the common good only in time of danger upon occasion of their private fears, in general looking simply to their own interest.

—PLUTARCH

I

Democracy: Justice and Inevitability

I. NEUTRALITY AND THE USE OF HISTORY

It is not uncommon for a major writer to be seen by his critics in widely divergent, even contradictory terms; Alexis de Tocqueville shares this fate. To the familiar causes of critical disagreement, Tocqueville added his own—a veil of neutrality or objectivity that concealed his deepest views. The publication in 1835 of the first part of *Democracy in America* thus gave rise to a still-continuing effort to discover Tocqueville's true intent: behind his facade of neutrality does he favor one social system, aristocracy or democracy, over the other?

Does he not, on the one hand, reveal in his writings the ingrained and inescapable bias of his aristocratic origins? Was he not hostile to the unformed and unforeseeable consequences of the democratic revolution? Did he not intend by his criticisms of the democratic system to "carry the reader to the point of wishing for its destruction"?[1] Was not the liberty he defended a "restricted liberty, protecting a small group of privileged people who were really independent so far as economic circumstances went"? Was it not "a liberty for believers, [a] liberty for owners . . . an aristocratic liberalism"?[2] Did he not believe that "the mass of men should remain bereft of political power"?[3]

Or did he not wish, on the other hand, that contemporary liberalism would "cease to be bourgeois and become democratic by admitting the masses to the suffrage"? Did he not regard the rise of a capitalist oligarchy as "the most revolting of all governments . . . a system offensive to his aristocratic instincts and to his democratic sympathies"?[4] Did he not, after all, "appreciate democracy as a form of progress in the providential control of history, the new political pattern [that] would be a blessing for most people"? Would not democratic political and social conditions "bring about the slow advance of the intellectual and cultural standards of modern societies through education, political action, and the application of religious ethics to the problems of social action"?[5]

Though it is impossible to ignore the extent to which Tocqueville's purported neutrality actually pervades his work, there can be no thought of denying his commitment to freedom, or his indefatigable promotion of the practices and institutions on which he believed a well-ordered democracy must rest. He saw no incompatibility in refusing to judge which of two social systems was superior, while at the same time striving to perfect the one destined to triumph. But his neutrality is our present concern.

So different are democracy and aristocracy, according to Tocqueville, that no common measure can serve as a standard of evaluation:

[Democracy and aristocracy] are like two distinct orders of human beings, each of which has its own merits and defects, its own advantages and its own evils. Care must therefore be taken not to judge the state of society that is now coming into existence by notions derived from a state of society that no longer exists; for as these states of society are exceedingly different in their structure, they cannot be submitted to a just or fair comparison.[6]

Instances in which he catalogs the advantages and disadvantages of each system, and so appears to lay the foundation for intelligent choice, do not mark a departure from his neutrality, for it is characteristic of him to remind the reader at such times that deliberation over the respective merits of aristocracy or democracy is superfluous and even irrelevant. What has made such deliberation irrelevant is the triumph of democracy, a triumph awesomely described in the introduction to the *Democracy*:

The various occurrences of national existence have everywhere turned to the advantage of democracy; all men have aided it by their exertions, both those who have intentionally labored in its cause and those who have served it unwittingly; those who have fought for it and even those who have declared themselves its opponents have all been driven along in the same direction, have all labored to one end; some unknowingly and some despite themselves, all have been blind instruments in the hands of God.[7]

It would be erroneous to dismiss these sentiments as youthful hyperbole. Not only are they retained in the twelfth edition (1848), the last to be corrected by Tocqueville himself; they are specifically called to the reader's attention in the preface Tocqueville added to that edition.[8] The same theme is repeated in *The Old Régime and the French Revolution* (1856), published some twenty years after the initial appearance of the *Democracy*: "All our contemporaries are driven on by a force that we may hope to regulate or curb, but cannot overcome . . . it is a force impelling them, sometimes gently, sometimes at headlong speed, to the destruction of aristocracy."[a] His refusal to judge between aristocracy and democracy thus appears as an act of deference to history; once history has pronounced judgment (success or inevitability constituting the criterion), one may only promote the alternatives compatible with the victorious social condition—democratic freedom or (if we are not mindful) democratic despotism.

[a] Tocqueville, *Old Régime*, p. xii. Before making this statement, Tocqueville remarks that "there can be no certainty about the future." The significance of this acknowledgment of the limits of prediction is discussed below, pp. 9–11.

Although Tocqueville attaches the utmost importance to the inevitable triumph of democracy, even making it the cause from which his work and almost all elements of contemporary society spring, he never completely explains why democracy is bound to triumph. The search for something equivalent to a philosophy of history in his writings has therefore been carried on as avidly, and in as many directions, as the search for his true intent.

Thus Mill, in his first review of the *Democracy*, confidently writes that Tocqueville "considers it an established truth, on the proof of which it is no longer necessary to insist, that the progress of democracy neither can nor ought to be stopped," and also that a "comprehensive survey of the series of changes composing the history of our race ... has taught to M. de Tocqueville that the movement towards democracy dates from the dawn of modern civilization, and has continued steadily advancing from that time."[9] But, a century later, Jack Lively maintains that Tocqueville did not base his inevitability thesis on

a scientific law or metaphysical pattern which would explain and justify the inevitable course of the future into democracy by pointing out the evident course of the past; nor did he see in the emergent democracy the proper destiny of man, the teleological function of humanity, brought into being by some all-conquering Progress. .... It was not History or Progress which rendered the emergence of some form of social democracy necessary, but certain psychological, social and economic conditions of contemporary society.[10]

Similar disagreements have arisen over how much weight and significance Tocqueville gave to the role of Providence in accounting for the inevitable triumph of democracy. Albert Salomon argues that Tocqueville regarded man as the agent responsible for fulfilling God's will as it was revealed in history: "The rise and the growth of the democratic movement points to the will of the Almighty in its irreversible process. . . . The wisdom of Providence illuminates the direction in which mankind moves. It leaves freedom of action for the fulfillment of these providential ends. The realization of these providential goals is entrusted to the responsibility of the human co-worker in the eternal process of creation."[b] To Edward Gargan, however, Tocqueville's appeal to Providence is more pragmatic than sacred: Tocqueville gave to the universal results of history a "providential cast." Even when he "sought the sacred support of Providence to give force to his observations, the test that he employed was a profane one: the presence in any historical process of that which is constant and cumulative in impact, the extensive evidence that a process in history was unfolding toward an ascertainable present and dimly known future."[11]

These are but a few of the diverse interpretations of Tocqueville's view of history. To determine which, if any, accurately expresses his thought is as difficult as deciding on his true sympathies in the conflict between aristocracy and democracy. In fact, whatever has given rise to the diversity of opinions about the one may be equally responsible for the diversity about the other. The same professed neutrality that I believe is ultimately responsible for our indecision about his true intent may also, I suggest, be responsible for the imprecision with which he has presented his conception of history, and hence for our failure to agree what that conception is. Tocqueville's understanding of history (the function it is made to serve as well as its meaning) and his neutrality *vis-à-vis* democracy and aristocracy are very closely related, and the failure to recognize their interrelation has often led to confusion about both. To understand the role

---

[b] Salomon, "Tocqueville's Philosophy of Freedom," p. 410. In a later article, Salomon remarks that after 1848 Tocqueville "began to question the truth of providential history." ("Tocqueville, 1959," pp. 467–68.)

history plays in Tocqueville's thought is to find the clue that discloses his unambiguous intent.

Consider the proof of the inevitability thesis offered in the opening pages of the *Democracy*. It is familiar enough. Tocqueville begins his analysis with a profound awareness of a revolutionary phenomenon in the affairs of men. He acknowledges that everyone is aware, at least in a vague way, of the democratic revolution, but cautions that not everyone sees it in the same light: "To some it appears to be novel but accidental, and as such they hope it may still be checked; to others it seems irresistible, because it is the most uniform, the most ancient, and the most permanent tendency that is to be found in history."[12] To those who think the revolution novel or accidental Tocqueville cites evidence to the contrary. In support of his contention that in every century of the modern era (i.e., from about the twelfth century on) the gap between lord and commoner has narrowed, and that it will soon be completely closed, he chronicles the forces that have been at work promoting equality of conditions: the opening of the ranks of the clergy to all; the growth of a legal system and the rise to positions of prominence of those who made it their special study; the spread of enlightenment and of commercial activity; the leveling effects of the kings' struggles with the nobles; the decline of feudal tenure. The evidence Tocqueville offers is drawn solely from French history since the Crusades; it takes on a quasi-universality only through an appeal to everyday observation: "Nor is this [revolution] peculiar to France. Wherever we look, we perceive the same revolution going on throughout the Christian world."[13]

To this evidence Tocqueville contributes a finding of his own: the recognition of the providential character of the revolution.

The gradual development of the principle of equality is, therefore, a providential fact. It has all the chief characteristics of such a fact: it is universal; it is lasting; it constantly eludes all human interference; and all events as well as all men contribute to its progress. . . .

If the men of our time should be convinced, by attentive observation and sincere reflection, that the gradual and progressive development of social equality is at once the past and the future of their history, this discovery alone would confer upon the change the sacred character of a divine decree. To attempt to check democracy would be in that case to resist the will of God; and the nations would then be constrained to make the best of the social lot awarded to them by Providence.[14]

That Tocqueville's exposition of facts should have moral and religious overtones is characteristic of his historical analysis. But he brings out these overtones without departing from his neutral position. So zealously does he guard his neutrality that in enumerating the "chief characteristics" that mark the development of equality he never refers to the wisdom or goodness of Providence; had these been included, a presumption in favor of democracy would necessarily have been indicated.[c] In their absence, it is all the more striking that he should equate resistance to democracy's progress with resistance to the will of God. What men's response to this trend should be is by no means self-evident. Should they bow graciously before the inevitable whether it is beneficent or not? Could the trend not be construed as a punishment for their sins, and ought they not, then, to pray for their forgiveness and its removal? Should they, perhaps, struggle valiantly in favor of a noble albeit moribund cause? Significantly, Tocqueville does not here address himself to these

[c] At the end of the *Democracy* (II, 351), Tocqueville emphasizes God's justice.

questions. Nothing is allowed to weaken the force of his contention that resistance to democracy is impious. His neutrality does not preclude him from arriving at a conclusion that
positively promotes democracy.

The providential character of the march toward equality
plays a decisive role in lending credence to the inevitability
thesis. In the absence of any direct revelation of the divine
intention in human affairs, Tocqueville draws an analogy
with the natural sciences: "It is not necessary that God himself should speak in order that we may discover the unques-
tionable signs of his will. It is enough to ascertain what is
the habitual course of nature and the constant tendency of
events. I know, without special revelation, that the planets
move in the orbits traced by the Creator's hand."[15] Tocqueville was not, of course, the first to make this analogy. Even
if we disregard the common objections to it based on the
dissimilarities of the natural and human spheres, we may
still have reservations about its applicability to history. The
planets have traversed the same orbits over the entire period
of man's recorded observations, thus providing a continuity
on which prediction may be based; human affairs struck out
in an entirely new direction at the beginning of the modern
era. If we are not to suspect that Tocqueville's predictions
may be confounded by similar discontinuities, we need some
assurance that nothing in the period preceding the present
militates against the eventual triumph of equality; we also
need assurance that the causes of discontinuity in the past
have been overcome.

Specifically, we need answers to such questions as these:
Was there any preparation in the pre-egalitarian epoch for
the development into equality that was to follow? Was it
an epoch with historical laws unrelated to those of the
modern period, or perhaps with no laws at all? Tocqueville
does not tell us. His reticence may be pardonable if, as

Lively maintains, Tocqueville's "concern with history was secondary to his analysis of contemporary politics,"[16] but it does not dispel our misgivings when the inevitability thesis itself is at issue. A trend that has arisen in modern times may terminate in modern times. History, if it displays any pattern at all, may be cyclical rather than linear. Tocqueville himself, at one point in the *Democracy*, warns the "friends of democracy" to be wary lest the growth of a manufacturing class be accompanied by a return to aristocracy and "a permanent inequality of conditions."[d] With this as a possibility, the inevitability and permanence of equality of conditions, of democracy, can scarcely be said to have been demonstrated.

Tocqueville does not claim prescience in regard to the whole of the future. Instances abound, even within the *Democracy*, in which he disclaims any such competence. As to whether the American federal government will increase its power over the state governments, for example, he remarks, "The future conceals the final result of this tendency and the events which may check, retard, or accelerate the changes I have described; I do not pretend to be able to remove the veil that hides them." On the difficulty of determining whether a large republic can long survive, he comments that "For my own part, I think it imprudent for men who are every day deceived in relation to the actual and the present, and often taken by surprise in the circumstances with which they are most familiar, to attempt to limit what is possible and to judge the future." While discussing the final outcome of the struggle between whites and Negroes in the South, he comments: "The human mind may succeed in tracing a wide circle, as it were, which includes the future; but within that circle chance rules, and eludes all our foresight. In every

[d] Tocqueville, *Democracy*, II, 171. Whether such a social order would feature a traditional class structure is not clear.

picture of the future there is a dim spot which the eye of the understanding cannot penetrate."[17] We may question whether these examples controvert his thesis. At first sight they do not, for they refer only to the dark area within that circle, an area whose circumference is defined by historical laws that man may comprehend. Even the reintroduction of slavery after a lapse of a thousand years may be viewed as a temporary aberration, incapable in itself of affecting or forestalling the ultimate triumph of equality.[e] But surely the dimensions of the dim spot, or rather the possibilities within it, are of decisive importance to the credibility of the inevitability thesis. If the unforeseeable can do no more than accelerate or retard the course of history, the inevitability thesis may still stand, although it may be somewhat shaken. But if such changes as the restoration of inequality of conditions through the effects of a capitalist revolution may come to pass, if the future contains radical surprises whose effects reach to the limits of the "fatal circle" itself, the thesis suffers a mortal blow.

Some hesitancy about the inevitability of equality is perceptible, then, even in the *Democracy*. When we turn to Tocqueville's private writings, his hesitancy becomes open and unreserved. In a letter to Mrs. Grote, in 1850, Tocqueville makes this confession:

I learn from history that not one of the men who witnessed the downfall of the religious and social organizations that have passed away was able to guess or even to imagine what would ensue. Yet, this did not prevent Christianity from succeeding . . . idolatry, servitude [from succeeding] slavery, the barbarians from taking the place of Roman civilization, and feudalism in turn [from] ejecting the barbarians. Each of these changes occurred without having been anticipated by any of the writers in

---

[e] See the *Democracy*, I, p. 371 and especially p. 397: "Slavery, now confined to a single tract of the civilized earth, attacked by Christianity as unjust and by political economy as prejudicial, and now contrasted with democratic liberty and the intelligence of our age, cannot survive."

the times immediately preceding these total revolutions. Who then can affirm that any one social system is essential, and that another is impossible?[18]

In the famous passage in his *Recollections* on the permanence of the institutions of private property, Tocqueville is grieved to admit that "what we call necessary institutions are often no more than institutions to which we have grown accustomed.... In matters of social constitution the field of possibilities is much more extensive than men living in their various societies are ready to imagine."[19] And in his anguished correspondence with Gobineau Tocqueville unfolds a picture of history in which there is no inexorable march of social conditions:

Do you really believe that by tracing the destiny of peoples along these [i.e., racist] lines you can truly clarify history? And that our knowledge about humans becomes more certain as we abandon the practice followed since the beginning of time by the many great minds who have searched to find the cause of human events in the influence of certain men, of certain emotions, of certain thoughts, and of certain beliefs?

If only your doctrine, without being better established than theirs, could serve mankind better! ... After, for some time, one has observed the way in which public affairs are conducted, do you think one can avoid the impression ... [that] the destiny of men, whether of individuals or of nations, depends on what they want to be?[20]

While such sentiments occur increasingly in the private papers of his later years, Tocqueville never altered the inevitability thesis in his published works, though he had many opportunities to amend or rescind it.

This is not the only paradox that confronts us in Tocqueville's thought. His public advocacy of a thesis implying that all men have been blind instruments in the fulfillment of God's design coexists uneasily with his abhorrence, equally public, of those "absolute systems which represent all the events of history as depending upon great first causes linked by the chain of fatality, and which, as it were, suppress men from the history of the human race."[21] Where he sought to reconcile these opinions he resorted to the kind of formulation with which he concludes the *Democracy*:

Providence has not created mankind entirely independent or entirely free. It is true that around every man a fatal circle is traced beyond which he cannot pass; but within the wide verge of that circle he is powerful and free; as it is with man, so with communities. The nations of our time cannot prevent the conditions of men from becoming equal, but it depends upon themselves whether the principle of equality is to lead them to servitude or freedom, to knowledge or barbarism, to prosperity or wretchedness.[22]

This position is deceptively convincing if it is mistaken for the commonplace that man is never altogether free, imprisoned as he is within the confines and limitations imposed on his will by, for example, the form and structure of his body. Tocqueville simply substitutes the cage of history or Providence for the cage of the body; he does not advance our knowledge of how men and nations may be both blind instruments in the hands of God and, within limits, free agents.

Nowhere in Tocqueville's work do we find more than a superficial account of how men may be both free and not free. The closest approximation to a satisfactory explanation occurs in the chapter in the *Democracy* on the distinguishing features of historians in democratic times.† Tocqueville contrasts two very different errors to which historians are prone: exaggerating the role of human freedom (common to both

---

† This chapter (II, Book 1, chap. xx), in which Tocqueville criticizes tendencies in other writers from which he himself is not altogether free, illustrates his own (perhaps deliberate) tendency to make statements that induce his readers to reflect on his own procedures. In the *Old Régime*, for example (p. 161), he rebukes those who, following a fashion he had foreseen in the *Democracy* (II, 79), see the hand of Providence in everything. He is similarly critical of the French addiction to general ideas, and even casts some doubt on his own usage of the term "equality" (*ibid.*, pp. 73–74).

ancient and aristocratic historians) and, contrariwise, reducing freedom to a mere illusion (characteristic of democratic historians). He reproves the ancients for not making sufficient use of general theories or historical systems, and the aristocrats for writing as though the actions of individuals could alone explain the course of history; but he concentrates on explicating the errors of the democratic historians of his own time. These are the writers who are unable to "discern and analyze the reasons that, acting separately on the will of each member of the community, concur in the end to produce movement in the whole mass." Thus these writers "are led to believe that this movement is involuntary and that societies unconsciously obey some superior force . . . ."[23] Some democratic historians see this superior force as a transcendent one standing above society (an "inflexible Providence"); others as a "blind necessity" with such earthly roots as racial or climatic factors. Whatever the case, "A cause sufficiently extensive to affect millions of men at once and sufficiently strong to bend them all together in the same direction may well seem irresistible; having seen that mankind does yield to it, the mind is close upon the inference that mankind cannot resist it."[24]

Tocqueville refuses to draw this inference, and maintains that in both aristocratic and democratic times general causes (e.g., the march of democracy) and particular ones (e.g., the will of individuals) are always operative, although their proportions vary. In democratic times, for example, individual influences are weaker than in aristocratic ones, but still exercise some influence on a nation's history. In the present period, however, the period associated with the democratic revolution, all men have by his own admission been but blind agents of God's will; to attribute free will to men during this period is meaningless.[*g*] All that he can plausibly

---

g Cf. the following: "To compel all men to follow the same course toward the same object is a human conception; to introduce infinite variety of action,

assert is that individuals may come to express their free will at some future time, but he can give no reason for assuming that what has been true up to now will cease to be so in the future. It would be strange to suppose that God would manipulate men for some six or seven hundred years in order to bring about a particular social condition and then once again permit them to exercise their human freedom. In fact, Tocqueville never makes this assumption. If we take the inevitability thesis seriously, the role of freedom in his conception of history is minimal; in this respect, Tocqueville does not differ from the democratic historians he criticizes.

Yet the final significance of Tocqueville's analysis of democratic historians lies not in his quarrels with them, nor in his crude attempts to justify his own position. In truth, there is no quarrel. He does little more here than reject the *consequences* of a view of history in which there is no room for free will: "If this doctrine of necessity, which is so attractive to those who write history in democratic ages, passes from authors to their readers till it infects the whole mass of the community and gets possession of the public mind, it will soon paralyze the activity of modern society and reduce Christians to the level of the Turks." Ancient historians, though they failed to appreciate the significance of general causes, are at least to be commended for teaching men "how to command"; democratic historians teach only "how to obey." The doctrines of Tocqueville's contemporaries are especially pernicious, since they serve to reinforce the feeling of helplessness that characterizes modern man. If not combated, these doctrines will frustrate the chief moral object of the men of Tocqueville's time, namely, "to raise the faculties of men, not to complete their prostration."[25] Never-

---

but so combined that all these acts lead in a thousand different ways to the accomplishment of one great design, is a divine conception." (Tocqueville, *Democracy*, II, 386–87.)

theless, the deleterious effect on society of a particular conception of history is no proof of its falsity; it may be true in spite of being harmful. Tocqueville, however, is satisfied to base his evaluation of this conception on his judgment of its consequences; he does not undertake to demonstrate its falsity. To have done so would have called his own inevitability thesis into question, or at least directed more attention to its ambiguities and inconsistencies than he wished.

It may be objected that the conflict between the implications of the inevitability thesis and Tocqueville's insistence that man is free was resolved when he adopted Mill's explication of the nature of free will and necessity, an explication that appeared (in Mill's *System of Logic*) just three years after the second and final part of the *Democracy* was published. Indeed, on reading the *System of Logic* Tocqueville wrote to Mill, "The distinction you make between necessity as you understand it and *irresistibleness*, fatalism, is a burst of light. It seems to me that you open there a neutral ground upon which the two opposing schools, or at least reasonable men from the two schools, could easily meet and understand each other."[26] Mill had distinguished what he called the doctrine of necessity, which was compatible with human freedom, from fatalism: "A Fatalist believes . . . not only that whatever is about to happen will be the infallible result of the causes which produce it (which is the true Necessitarian doctrine) but, moreover, that there is no use struggling against it; that it will happen however we may strive to prevent it."[27] In other words, though the necessitarian acknowledges that every effect has a cause, he is prepared to argue that the exercise of free choice is itself a cause of the same rank as any other. However, it seems clear that according to Mill's distinction Tocqueville's own conception of the progress of democracy is fatalistic rather than necessitarian, at least as the conception is formulated in the introduction to the *Democracy* and reaffirmed (as we have seen) in the *Old Régime*. The idea that no human action can prevail against the course of history is the essence of fatalism, and it is this idea that occupies the forefront of Tocqueville's view of the development of equality. He even confides that he is writing the *Democracy* under a kind of "religious awe" produced "by the view of that irresistible revolution which has advanced for centuries in spite of every obstacle, and which is still advancing in the midst of the ruins it has caused."[28]

Even as Tocqueville never chose to publicly reveal his private doubts about the inevitability thesis, so he never chose to purge the thesis of its fatalistic aspects. On the contrary, five years after Mill's *Logic* appeared he reaffirmed those aspects in a new edition of the *Democracy*, and noted that the original work had been written "with a mind constantly occupied by a single thought—that the advent of democracy as a governing power in the world's affairs, *universal and irresistible*, was at hand."[29]

So it appears that the paradoxes in Tocqueville's writings cannot be explained away by alluding to a "change of view" that he may have undergone over the years.[h] Nor can it be maintained that Tocqueville was not cognizant of those paradoxes. He asserts the inevitability of the triumph of democracy in his major published works, the *Democracy* in his youth, the *Old Régime* in his maturity. He expresses doubts concerning this same victory of democracy, principally in works not intended for publication, such as his *Recollections*, and in private correspondence. We cannot, then, exclude the possibility that his failure to amend his published views was deliberate, that he simply did not wish to clear up the am-

---

[h] In the *Old Régime* (pp. xiv–xv), after reproducing views he held at the time of the *Democracy*, Tocqueville adds, "Such were my views and thus I wrote twenty years ago, and nothing that has taken place in the world since then has led me to change my mind." If he *had* changed his mind, at least he was not anxious to publicize the fact.

biguities within his work. This apparently strange behavior can be explained if it can be shown that in Tocqueville's mind the thesis he advanced for public consumption was meant to edify; that to Tocqueville this thesis, whatever its truth, was good for men to believe in; that he believed mankind, were they only to take his thesis as fact, would straightway turn toward improving their lot within the context of democracy rather than dissipating their energies in a struggle to revive an unjust social system.

Tocqueville's apparent neutrality between democracy and aristocracy did not preclude, as John Stuart Mill expressed it, "the deepest and steadiest concern for all the great interests, material and spiritual, of the human race." Tocqueville is "anything but indifferent to the ends to which all forms of government profess to be means." His achievement was to have combined this deep concern with a perfectly balanced sense of scientific objectivity: "When M. de Tocqueville says that he studied America not in order to disparage or to vindicate democracy, but in order to understand it, he makes no false claim to impartiality. Not a trace of prejudice, or so much as a previous leaning ... shows itself in his work. ... Between aristocracy and democracy he holds the balance straight, with all the impassibility of a mere scientific observer."[30]

It is precisely Tocqueville's devotion to the "great interests" that makes his neutrality all the more incomprehensible. Unless democracy and aristocracy are equally compatible with the material and spiritual requirements of mankind (something he does not attempt to prove), it is difficult to see how his neutrality could have been maintained, much less defended. To know the proper ends of man, to ascertain which social condition facilitates and which frustrates the fulfillment of this or that end, and then to adopt an air of indifference would reveal not only an extraordinary degree of scientific impassibility, but an equal degree of moral obtuseness. It seems safe to say that such a charge ought not to be presumptuously leveled at Tocqueville. In fact, it has been charged that his moral sensibilities threatened his dispassionate search after truth. His correspondence with Gobineau is well-known enough so that we need not refer to it here to support the thesis that Tocqueville was not as interested in the "philosophical merits of an idea" as in its "moral or political effects."[31] Moreover, to emphasize an idea's truth at the expense of its moral and political effects would be to confuse the requirements of theory with those of practice—a mistake Tocqueville was hardly likely to have made. I shall say more about Tocqueville's ideas on the relationship of theory and practice below.

To allege that Tocqueville was prepared to urge men to acquiesce to democracy simply because it had succeeded the aristocratic social system, or was in the process of succeeding it, would be to charge him not only with another inconsistency, but with gross moral hypocrisy as well. Consider the objections Tocqueville himself makes to the Hegelian identification of what is with what is right: "[Hegel's] doctrines asserted that in a political sense all established facts ought to be submitted to as legitimate, and that the very circumstance of their existence was sufficient to make obedience to them a duty. . . . From this Pandora's box have escaped all sorts of moral diseases from which the people [are] still suffering."[32] Moreover, from other portions of his correspondence we learn that even if the evidence for the inevitability of equality were altogether incontrovertible, Tocqueville would not necessarily acquiesce—he might still prefer to sacrifice himself for a noble if moribund cause. Thus he writes to Mrs. Grote, "It is . . . the duty of honest people to stand up for the only system which they understand, and even to die for it if a better be not shown to them."[33] And to Corcelle, Tocqueville wholly rejects success as a criterion for obedience: "I rejoice to find, as time goes on, that I am not one of those who naturally bow before success. The more a cause seems to be abandoned, the more passionately I become attached to it."[34] Yet how may we reconcile these sentiments with the text of the *Democracy* where Tocqueville equates disobedience to the unfolding course of human history with impiety? What Tocqueville is not prepared to do himself he recommends, even makes mandatory, for others. The charge of hypocrisy cannot be obviated unless it can be shown that he believed the cause before which he would have men bow was itself just, and not only just, but salutary also. If he believed the end just, he doubtless also believed that to propagate a thesis designed to bring that end to pass was a socially beneficent and morally worthy act, even if the thesis itself was false.[35]

It is only by virtue of the hypothesis that the thesis is meant to serve a just end that the various paradoxes that surround it may be resolved, and Tocqueville's deliberate failure to resolve them be explained. The inevitability thesis was free from the evils of the Hegelian Pandora's box because a democratic revolution would, if properly controlled and directed, bring about a social and political system that was intrinsically just, independent of any vindication through the historical process. The inevitability thesis, then, is a salutary myth, and the propagation of salutary myths is wholly consistent with other strains of Tocqueville's thought, most notably with his defense of spiritualistic myths designed to restrain certain unwholesome features of democracy.[36]

Tocqueville writes with full consciousness of the requirements of political practice; his first consideration is always the effect his thought will have on society. It is as a statesman writing for statesmen that Tocqueville is to be understood. If he does not develop his position to the degree and with the precision appropriate to a philosophic treatise, it is because his readers do not require him to:

The habits of mind that are suited to an active life are not always suited to a contemplative one. The man of action is frequently obliged to content himself with the best he can get because he would never accomplish his purpose if he chose to carry every detail to perfection. He has occasion perpetually to rely on ideas that he has not had leisure to search to the bottom, *for he is much more frequently aided by the seasonableness of an idea than by its strict accuracy, and in the long run he risks less in making use of some false principles than in spending his time in establishing all his principles on the basis of truth.* The world is not led by long or learned demonstrations; a rapid glance at particular incidents, the daily study of the fleeting passions of the multitude, the accidents of the moment, and the art of turning them to account decide all its affairs.[37]

Tocqueville brought to his contemplative tasks the habits of mind suited to an active life; that is, it was primarily in the light of the requirements of political life that he undertook his contemplative tasks. He sought to resolve the main political conflict of his own time (and perhaps of all time), the conflict that arises from the question of whether society may be most justly ruled by the few or the many. His method was to temper political passions already fevered. To attempt a frontal defense of democracy as the only just social system would, in such circumstances, have only exacerbated the differences between the democrats and the aristocrats, the immediate addressees of his work. By assigning the defense of democracy to history or Providence, he removed himself from the partisan fray.

The inevitability thesis is, then, the shield behind which he can maintain his neutrality, a neutrality that is not only compatible with the cause of democracy, but actively promotes it. Whatever undermines the inevitability thesis undermines his neutrality and the cause of democracy as well. For these reasons, Tocqueville did not remove from his formulation of the thesis such ambiguities as we have explored; for these reasons, also, the inevitability thesis is the most conspicuous premise of his published works. Perhaps we have only to take seriously what Tocqueville himself said of his enterprise in a letter to his friend Eugène Stoffels, a month after the first part of the *Democracy* was published:

I tried to diminish the ardor of [the Republican party], and without discouraging them, to show them the only road to take. I attempted to diminish the terrors of [the aristocrats], *and to bend their will to the idea of an inevitable future* in such a way that the one being less impetuous, and the others offering less resistance, society could advance more perfectly toward the necessary realization of its destiny. Here is the master idea of the work.[4]

II. THE JUSTIFICATION OF DEMOCRACY

Tocqueville's neutral position between democracy and aristocracy did not strike every observer as favorably as it did Mill. Paul Janet, writing just after Tocqueville's death, criticized Tocqueville for having occupied himself overmuch with questions of fact and having brushed aside questions of right: "He [Tocqueville] examined what are historically the good or bad consequences, happy or unhappy, of democracy. He did not try to find out if democracy, taken by itself, is a just cause."[38] But Janet was wrong: Tocqueville did undertake to answer the "question of right," and his answer, almost all appearances to the contrary notwithstanding, was

---

[4] Tocqueville to Eugène Stoffels, Feb. 21, 1835, in *Oeuvres Complètes* (Beaumont), V, 426–27. The original is perhaps stronger than the translation conveys: "J'ai cherché à diminuer les terreurs des seconds et *à plier leur volonté sous l'idée d'un avenir inévitable.*" (Italics mine.)

not one of obsequious deference to the verdict of history. Curiously, it was not significantly different from Janet's conclusion that "Democracy, taken by itself, is a just cause. Popular sovereignty and equality of conditions are principles that can be abused, corrupted, badly understood, and badly applied, but in the end they are legitimate principles, good by themselves, and a society founded on them is superior, everything else being equal, to societies founded on opposite principles."[39] However much Tocqueville tended to conceal his evaluation of democracy, the legitimacy of the principle of equality was the starting point of his reflections and the occasion for his inquiry into the abiding needs of mankind. To the proof of this statement I shall now turn.[j]

The grand alternative to democracy in Tocqueville's writings is, of course, aristocracy, a social system based on the inequality of man. Every reader of the *Democracy* is struck by the apparently contradictory attitudes Tocqueville adopts toward the social condition of the old regime. On the one hand, he uses aristocracy as a standard against which to measure the democratic social condition, and against this standard, democracy is usually found wanting. Aristocracy evokes man's highest spiritual qualities: his attachment to causes beyond himself, his cultivation of the arts and sciences, his pursuit of enterprises of surpassing grandeur, and his love of fine manners, beauty, and poetry. On the other hand, Tocqueville recognizes that aristocracy cannot serve

---

[j] The omission, in what follows, of any discussion of the relevance of Christianity may seem strange inasmuch as the most prominent justification for democracy in Tocqueville's writings appears to be theological in character. Yet Tocqueville does not undertake to prove that Christianity is compatible with democracy alone, and that democracy thus has the status of the only just political order. On the contrary, Tocqueville argues that Christianity is either apolitical or transpolitical, and is compatible with virtually any social or political system. (See p. 50 below; also *Democracy*, II, 24.) There is, of course, no denying that Tocqueville invokes religion in resolving the problem of democracy. But to argue that democracy needs the ministrations of a religion is not to prove that only in religion can democracy find its justification.

as such a standard: "The question is not how to reconstruct aristocratic society, but how to make liberty proceed out of that democratic state of society in which God has placed us."[40] Tocqueville's ambivalence toward aristocracy is consistent with an unequivocal rejection of its origins: he admires the flower but abhors the seed from which it grows. Thus, despite his claim at the close of the *Democracy* that democracy and aristocracy are fundamentally incommensurable, he does in fact subject them to common standards, standards that are trans-historical, that transcend the limitations of any particular social or political condition. Weighed against these standards, aristocracy is found wanting in that it violates certain clear precepts of natural justice.

Tocqueville's approach to the problem of aristocracy is prefigured in this passage on aristocratic society from the introduction to the *Democracy*:

The people, never having conceived the idea of a social condition different from their own, and never expecting to become equal to their leaders, received benefits from them without discussing their rights. They . . . submitted to their exactions . . . as to the inevitable visitations of the Deity. . . . As the noble never suspected that anyone would attempt to deprive him of the privileges which he believed to be legitimate, and as the serf looked upon his own inferiority as a consequence of the immutable order of nature, it is easy to imagine that some mutual exchange of good will took place between two classes so differently endowed by fate. Inequality and wretchedness were then to be found in society, but the souls of neither rank of men were degraded.[41]

The salutary state of society rested on certain beliefs or opinions about fate, Providence, and the legitimacy of the regime shared by commoners and nobles alike. Tocqueville emphasizes that it is opinion, not reality, that is important: "Men are not corrupted by the exercise of power or debased by the habit of obedience, but by the exercise of a power which they *believe* to be illegitimate, and by obedience to a rule which they *consider* to be usurped and oppressive."[k] Whether or not this is true need not concern us here. However, the opinions that made aristocratic society livable must be re-examined in the light of Tocqueville's demonstration that the intent of the Deity had been misread. What had been thought part of the "immutable order of nature" proved only a passing stage in the inexorable march toward equality. Those who gave their allegiance to aristocratic society in the belief that it was permanent and providential were—as it turned out—mistaken. They erred in believing that God destined no alternative to aristocracy. Thus Tocqueville thrusts this question upon us: did the serfs also err in be-lieving aristocracy to be legitimate, neither oppressive in its rule nor originating in usurpation?

Tocqueville's judgment of aristocracy is only gradually disclosed in the *Democracy*. In the introduction he observes that "the nobles, placed high as they were above the peo-ple, could take that calm and benovolent interest in their fate which the shepherd feels toward his flock...."[42] This highly favorable judgment is qualified later:

When an aristocracy governs, those who conduct the affairs of state are exempted, by their very station in society, from any want: content with their lot, power and renown are the *only* objects for which they strive; placed far above the obscure crowd, they do not always clearly perceive how the well-being of the mass of the people will redound to their own grandeur. They are not, indeed, callous to the sufferings of the poor; but they cannot feel those miseries as acutely as if they were them-selves partakers of them.[43]

---

[k] *Ibid.*, I, 9 (italics mine). For Albert Salomon, Tocqueville is the originator of the theory of "images and counter-images" to explain the operation of ruling and being ruled in society. See his "Tocqueville, 1959," pp. 460–61.

"Provided that the people appear to submit to their lot," the nobles take no further interest in improving their subjects' condition. Democracies tend to promote the interests of the people, but aristocracies have a "natural defect," a "capital fault," of tending to "work for themselves and not for the people.[44] With this judgment Tocqueville actually reverses his initial assessment: now, aristocratic shepherds are simply indifferent toward their charges, and incapable of perceiving the true condition of the people: "The men who compose [an aristocratic caste] do not resemble the mass of their fellow citizens; they do not think or feel in the same manner, and they scarcely believe that they belong to the same race. They cannot, therefore, thoroughly understand what others feel nor judge of others by themselves. ... Feudal institutions awakened a lively sympathy for the sufferings of certain men, but none at all for the miseries of mankind."[45]

The relatively mild terms in which Tocqueville's judgment of aristocracy is put, as well as its gradual disclosure, may be understood when it is recalled that aristocrats constituted an important segment of his audience. Intent upon winning them over to the cause of perfecting democracy, Tocqueville reveals his true feelings somewhat obliquely. Thus he reserves his most forthright indictment of aristocracy for the chapter that concludes the first part of the *Democracy*, a chapter that rather resembles an appendix to the main body of the work and that might easily be bypassed by the casual reader. Its title, "The Present and Probable Future Condition of the Three Races that Inhabit the Territory of the United States," scarcely conveys the full scope of its contents. For the racial problem in America is not the sole theme of the chapter; with a slight shift in perspective, the theme serves as a vehicle for a defense of the principle of equality.

As Tocqueville sees it, the inequalities that prevailed in the Middle Ages were solely a creation of law, of conventional law. "Nothing can be more fictitious than a purely legal inferiority, nothing more contrary to the instinct of mankind than these permanent divisions established between beings evidently similar." But discrimination by whites against Negroes in America, though supported by law, appears to him to be grounded in something more substantial: "Among the moderns the abstract and transient fact of slavery is fatally united with the physical and permanent fact of color." Tocqueville recites his contemporaries' conventions about the Negro: "We scarcely acknowledge the common features of humanity in this stranger whom slavery has brought among us. His physiognomy is to our eyes hideous, his understanding weak, his tastes low; and we are almost inclined to look upon him as a being intermediate between man and the brutes."[46] Yet there can be no escaping the fact that Tocqueville dissociates himself from his contemporaries, here as in so many other instances. "The moderns," he tells us, " . . . have three prejudices to contend against . . . the prejudice of the master, the prejudice of the race, and the prejudice of color."[l] To Tocqueville, the situation in the South is "the order of nature overthrown."[47] He was no more sanguine of the restoration of the natural order in the United States, as far as the races were concerned, than was Jefferson before him. Inequalities originating solely in conventional law are difficult enough to eradicate; Tocqueville despairs of seeing the end of those that "seem to be based upon the immutable laws of Nature herself." What Nature had apparently done, in the American instance, was

---

[l] Tocqueville, *Democracy*, I, 372. Richard Resh accuses Tocqueville of "neo-racist views," but Resh fails to appreciate the difference between Tocqueville's own views and those he represents his contemporaries as holding. (Resh, pp. 251–59.)

to facilitate the formation of an aristocracy based on "visible and indelible signs."[48] Lest there be any doubt as to the significance *he* attaches to these signs, Tocqueville unequivocally declares later in the chapter that every aristocracy (hence also one originating in color differences), is unnatural and unjust:

An aristocratic body is composed of a certain number of citizens who, without being very far removed from the mass of the people, are nevertheless permanently stationed above them . . . . Nothing can be imagined more contrary to nature and to the secret instincts of the human heart than a subjection of this kind. . . . Aristocratic institutions cannot exist without laying down the inequality of men as a fundamental principle, legalizing it beforehand and introducing it into the family as well as into society; but these are things so repugnant to natural equity that they can only be extorted from men by force.

I do not think a single people can be quoted, since human society began to exist, which has, by its own free will and its own exertions, created an aristocracy within its own bosom. All the aristocracies of the Middle Ages were founded by military conquest; the conqueror was the noble, the vanquished became the serf. Inequality was then imposed by force; and after it had once been introduced into the manners of the country, it maintained itself and passed naturally into the laws.[49]

When Tocqueville contrasts aristocratic with democratic liberty in his article "France Before the Revolution" (written just after the first part of the *Democracy*), he reiterates this declaration. Aristocratic liberty is justified by those enjoying it as a privilege accruing to particular individuals or groups; democratic liberty, on the contrary, is a right originating in the common humanity of man. Of democratic liberty, Tocqueville writes:

According to the modern concept, the democratic, and I venture to say the true, concept of liberty, each man, being presumed to have received from nature the necessary intelligence to conduct his own life, derives from birth an equal and indefeasible right to live uncontrolled by his fellows in all that concerns his own affairs, and to regulate as he wishes his own destiny.

From the moment when this notion of liberty has penetrated deeply into the minds of the people, and has solidly established itself there, absolute and arbitrary power is thenceforth but a usurpation or an accident; for if no one is under any moral obligation to submit to another, it follows that the sovereign will can rightfully emanate only from the union of the wills of all.[50]

Only that regime is legitimate in which political obligation arises from the consent of each man. Tocqueville agrees with the modern tradition that all regimes are conventional in origin; no man is by nature under any obligation to submit to the rule of another. But this understanding of legitimacy, which Tocqueville puts forward not as just another opinion but rather as the truth about political obligation, cannot but alter the moral perspective within which he views ruling and being ruled. It alters as well the perspective of the rulers and the ruled. If, as Tocqueville claims, men are debased only by obedience to a rule they regard as illegitimate, men may remain loyal to an aristocracy without having their souls corrupted only if they remain ignorant of the aristocracy's true origins. But neither ignorance nor the self-respect dependent on it is possible any longer. Tocqueville has not only shown that God destined an alternative to aristocracy, but he has also torn the veil of time, law, and tradition from aristocracy's origins. In principle, at least, no course is open but to embrace democracy.

Against the argument that Tocqueville himself so embraces democracy three principal objections may be raised. First, that this argument obscures Tocqueville's assignment to aristocracy of an important role in fulfilling several paramount political responsibilities, notably the preservation of freedom and the initiation of glorious tasks. Second, that it assumes that Tocqueville's remarks on aristocracy have, and were meant to have, the force of judgments rather than of mere descriptions. Finally, that it takes a judgment on feudal aristocracy—if, indeed, a judgment is made—as applying to aristocracy simply. The first two objections may be treated briefly; the last will require more extensive analysis.

Tocqueville is surely not indifferent to the cultural accomplishments of aristocracy, but he reserves his most extravagant praise for its political contributions to a state: glory, power, and the protection of freedom. Glory entails operations on a vast scale extending over a long period of time, tasks traditionally held to be within the compass only of an aristocracy. As to the protection of freedom, aristocrats, situated between the people and their natural oppressor, the monarch, had always been in the forefront of the defense against tyranny. Tocqueville could not conceal his astonishment that the French nobility, on the eve of the Revolution, was unable to offer any defense in its own behalf:

[None of the nobles] had ever considered by what means an aristocracy may justify its privileges in the eyes of the people. They did not know what to say in order to show that only an aristocracy can preserve the people from the oppression of royal tyranny and from the miseries of revolution; that the privileges which seem established in the sole interest of those who possess them do also form the best guarantee for the tranquillity and prosperity even of those who do not have them.[51]

Tocqueville thus purports to present a defense of aristocracy familiar to a few and likely to be successful "in the eyes of the people"; but he characteristically does not indicate whether he himself finds this defense convincing. Moreover, it would be an error to conclude that he believes aristocracy indispensable, for one of his most prominent themes is that its place may be filled in democratic times by voluntary associations, both social and political. These protect individuals against encroachments by the state (the modern analogue to the monarch), and provide that continuity in space and time thought to be an exclusive attribute of an aristocracy. It is essential to any society that these functions be served, but they need not be served by an aristocracy.

The second objection is that Tocqueville's professed neutrality is not violated if his observations on aristocracy are understood to be merely descriptive. It may be alleged that he treats the old regime as he does American democracy, that is, by delineating its "natural consequences" without passing any judgment.[52] Yet Tocqueville's descriptions are not free of judgments. Thus he writes of the "capital fault" of an aristocracy, and of its "natural defects." The misery to which the majority of the people are consigned is not merely an abstraction for him, and he is not prepared to accept their misery as an inescapable condition of human existence. His correspondence with Gobineau, for example, indicates how conscious he was of the need to improve the lot of the majority, and of the means necessary to do it.[53] In addition, Tocqueville is contemptuous of many so-called aristocratic virtues. Those peculiar to feudal aristocracy he labels "fantastic notions," declaring that the aristocrats "would not hesitate to invert the natural order of conscience in order to give these virtues precedence over all others. It may even be conceived that some of the more bold and brilliant vices would readily be set above the quiet, unpretending virtues." One virtue, military courage, was exalted above all others "even at the expense of reason and humanity."[54] In view of these explicit pronouncements, it would be truer to say of aristocracy than of democracy that Tocqueville by his criticisms sought to "carry the reader to the point of wishing for its destruction."

The substance of the third objection is that Tocqueville's criticisms are indeed evaluative, but are meant to apply only to decadent aristocracies, those that manage to tighten their grip on privilege while renouncing any responsibility for the maintenance of order, the administration of justice, or the conduct of national affairs. For an aristocracy that remains alive to its responsibilities Tocqueville has, as noted above, a high regard indeed. In the *Old Régime*, for example, he writes that "when the nobles had real power as well as privileges, when they governed and administrated, their rights could be at once greater and less open to attack." He deplores the fact that the nobility was finally eliminated from the life of the nation instead of "being forced to bow to the rule of law . . . since thereby the nation was deprived of a vital part of its substance, and a wound that time will never heal was inflicted on our national freedom."[55] But the aristocrats Tocqueville primarily has in mind throughout the *Democracy* are the feudal lords of the Middle Ages and their French descendants who had effectively ceased to govern. Can it be maintained that a judgment on these nobles applies to the whole institution of aristocracy?

Tocqueville often supports the idea that the form of aristocracy prevailing in the feudal era was a deviation from, or an exception to, some ideal form. In the *Old Régime*, in particular, he distinguishes between a caste and an aristocracy proper.[56] The latter is composed of all the "leading men" in a community, who serve primarily as a governing body. A caste too may serve as a governing body, but admission to it is exclusively dependent on birth, irrespective of any talent for the exercise of leadership. French practice exemplifies the caste system. The English, on the other hand, overcame the disposition to caste practices inherent in the feudal system and worked their way back to a genuine aristocracy ("In England alone has aristocracy returned").[57] Even in the *Democracy* Tocqueville is not unmindful of a pure form of aristocracy in contrast to the feudal system. Speaking of the western settlements of America, he remarks that "in this part of the American continent . . . the population has escaped the influence not only of great names [i.e., of birth] and great wealth, but even of the natural aristocracy of knowledge and virtue."[58]

There are, then, three principal types of aristocracy: a natural aristocracy of virtue and talent, a caste system exemplified by the French, and an English variant somewhere between the other two. Yet all suffer from the corruption of interest, the first no less than the others, and hence none of them is unqualifiedly just. The case of natural aristocracy is especially significant, for what applies to it applies even more so to the others. The claim of the wise and the good to rule cannot be elevated to an exclusive principle of legitimacy, for no group of men, whatever their talents, can be relied on in all cases to put other men's interests above their own: "It is no doubt of importance to the welfare of nations that they should be governed by men of talents and virtue; but it is perhaps still more important for them that the interests of those men should not differ from the interests of the community at large; for if such were the case, their virtues might become almost useless and their talents might be turned to a bad account."[59] From this all too human defect no aristocracy, not even that of the English (which most approximates the natural rule of the wise and virtuous), is wholly free. In his notes on his journey to England, Tocqueville's indictment is without reservation; in the *Democracy*, two years later, his views are put more moderately, but nonetheless remain the same:

The English aristocracy is perhaps the most liberal that has ever existed . . . no body of men has ever, uninterruptedly, furnished so many honorable and enlightened individuals to the government of a country. It cannot escape observation, however, that in the legislation of England the interests of the poor have often been sacrificed to the advantages of the rich, and the rights of the majority to the privileges of a few. The result is that England at the present day combines the extremes of good and evil fortune in the bosom of her society; and the miseries and privations of her poor almost equal her power and renown.[60]

For Tocqueville it is self-evident that this must be the case; he considers it axiomatic "that democracy annoys one part of the community and that aristocracy oppresses another."[61] Furthermore, he argues that a regime that oppresses the greater part of the community cannot escape opprobrium by appealing to its allegedly superior competence in the art of government. Aristocracy may be more expert at legislation, but if its laws, however efficient, favor the interest of the minority at the expense of the majority, those laws promote an end that is evil. Democratic legislation is a different matter; Tocqueville credits it with furthering the well-being of the majority:

Democratic laws generally tend to promote the welfare of the greatest possible number; for they emanate from the majority of the citizens, who are subject to error, but who cannot have an interest opposed to their own advantage. The laws of an aristocracy tend, on the contrary, to concentrate wealth and power in the hands of the minority, because an aristocracy, by its very nature, constitutes a minority. In may therefore be asserted, as a general proposition, that the purpose of a democracy in its legislation is more useful to humanity than that of an aristocracy.[62]

Tocqueville appeals to a kind of invisible hand to explain this principle's operation even in the absence of responsible and competent rulers: "There is, indeed, a secret tendency in democratic institutions that makes the exertions of the citizens subservient to the prosperity of the community in spite of their vices and mistakes; while in aristocratic institutions there is a secret bias which, notwithstanding the talents and virtues of those who conduct the government, leads them to contribute to the evils that oppress their fellow creatures."[63]

Although Tocqueville's judgment of aristocracy in the *Democracy* is stated in universal terms and hence covers all three types of aristocracy, he thought of the French example as most nearly approximating aristocracy's essence: rule transmissible exclusively by birth. He did not regard a natural aristocracy as a "true" aristocracy because its distinguishing characteristics were not without exception "capable of transmission from father to son."[64] Nor could he look on the English form as other than unique; he refused to judge aristocracy "theoretically" from its example.[65] To comprehend the nature of aristocracy as Tocqueville understood it, one must turn to France. As Seymour Drescher has noted, "Regarding the characteristics defined as more ideally aristocratic, the Continental, or more specifically the French nobility [provided] the obvious models."[66] Thus Tocqueville's judgment of the aristocracy of the old regime, an aristocracy of birth, is his judgment of aristocracy itself.

If we can agree, then, that Tocqueville anticipated a democratic substitute for aristocracy's role in preserving freedom, that his description of aristocracy is indeed evaluative, and that his judgment on the nobility of the old regime may be taken for his judgment on all aristocracy, we may also agree that Tocqueville did attempt a justification of democracy, and may then proceed to examine the roots of that justification.

In appealing as he does to considerations of natural equity, Tocqueville invokes a standard transcending time, place, and condition. Yet his thought is deeply imbued with a sense of the temporal and the historical: a specific social condition has arisen in modern times that facilitates insight into the standard itself. There is an openness about democracy and democratic conditions that rather readily reveals the true nature of man. Aristocracy and aristocratic manners, on the contrary, "conceal the natural man." They throw "a pleasing illusory charm over human nature." Strip man of such finery and he will be seen as he really is: closer to the brute, perhaps, but closer to his real nature. Tocqueville argues: "Among a democratic people . . . the form and the substance of human actions . . . often stand in closer relation [than among aristocrats], and if the great picture of human life is less embellished, it is more true."[m] What applies to manners "properly so called," that is, to matters of taste, applies as well to virtues or to mores, the habits and opinions that make up the moral and intellectual condition of a people.[67] When the democratic revolution has completely triumphed, man's virtues and manners will be in exact correspondence with his true nature. The democratic revolution, accompanied as it is by the gradual disappearance of aristocratic forms, is thus the agency by which man's nature is revealed. Inquiry into the nature of democratic man is inquiry into the nature of man per se.

It is Tocqueville's understanding of the nature of man, particularly the moral requirements of his nature, that provides his ultimate justification for democracy. He believed he had perceived man's nature directly, through his examination of men and mores in democratic America, as well as indirectly, through his reconstruction of the genesis of morality. This reconstruction is the theme of his chapter on

---

[m] Tocqueville, *Democracy*, II, 230–31. Cf. the similar sentiment in Rousseau's *First Discourse*: "Richness of apparel may proclaim the man of fortune, and elegance the man of taste; but true health and manliness are known by different signs. . . . Before art had moulded our behavior, and taught our passions to speak an artificial language, our morals were rude but natural." (Rousseau, p. 148.)

honor in the *Democracy*; and that chapter is also the source of his most complete and compelling theoretical justification of democracy.

According to Tocqueville, there are two distinct sources for the moral judgments men make of their fellows: "At one time they judge them by those simple notions of the just and the unjust which are diffused all over the world; at another they appraise them by a few very special rules which belong exclusively to some particular age and country." When these special rules make up a coherent whole they constitute a code of honor, which is "simply that peculiar rule, founded upon a peculiar state of society, by the application of which a people or a class allot praise or blame." Such a code often conceals, frequently overcomes, but never quite eradicates a second source of morality: a "more general, more ancient, and more holy law," coeval with man himself, which men feel by a "dim but mighty instinct."[68] This law is variously equated with the "natural order of conscience," the "general principles of right and wrong," the "moral laws adopted by the mass of mankind," or the "general reason and the universal conscience of mankind."[69] With the advent of equality of conditions, the general and universal conscience begins to be felt as a primary source of public morality. The democratic condition does not so much alter man's nature as bring it to the fore, and allow and encourage it to express itself.

The standards of justice and injustice prescribed by the general conscience of mankind are themselves not primary, but derived from the wants, necessities, and interests of man as a natural being. "Mankind is subject to general and permanent wants that have created moral laws, to the neglect of which men have ever and in all places naturally attached the notion of censure and shame. To infringe these laws was *to do ill*; *to do well* was to conform to them." The prohibition against murder is an element of this natural moral code.

It derives its justification, as far as Tocqueville is here concerned, not from divine law or compassion for one's fellow man, but rather from the recognition that "it is the general and permanent interest of mankind that men should not kill each other." One can scarcely avoid speculating about occasions when the general interest of mankind may seem to conflict with the immediate needs of a particular people. Tocqueville's illustrations suggest that such occasions are often the rule rather than the exception. Though murder is contrary to the general code, "It may happen to be the peculiar and temporary interest of a people or a class to justify or even to honor homicide." According to feudal morality, "Some of the actions which were indifferent on the part of a man in humble life dishonored a noble." But the idea of evaluating an action by the status of its perpetrator, without considering the intrinsic character of the act itself, is "repugnant to the general conscience of mankind." Feudal society, it will be recalled, inverted the "natural order of conscience" to give military courage precedence over all other virtues. Americans, too, make a similar inversion; owing to the "peculiar and temporary wants of the American community," they encourage acquisitiveness, a trait censurable by universal standards.[70]

Tocqueville does not deny that conditions may arise that necessitate such perversions of natural morality. A failure on the part of the Americans to laud commercial virtues might well be "fatal" to them. The feudal class in Europe similarly depended on its code of honor for its existence. But to him such urgent necessities, and the requirements of such unique situations, are morally irrelevant: the foundation of true morality must be the same for all men everywhere.[71]

[71] Tocqueville, *Democracy*, II, 248, 244–45. Tocqueville applied this concept in his resolution of the problem of what restrictions, if any, may be placed upon the majority. There is a revealing juxtaposition of two observations in his notebooks for the *Democracy*: the first takes note of the fact that in America the

In every society up to the present, Tocqueville argues, natural justice has given way to a system of morality reflecting the particular needs of the society or catering to the privileged ruling groups within it. With the disappearance of these groups' privileges, with the gradual extinction of the unequal conditions from which privilege arises and which in turn sustain it, these "secondary" moral systems will also disappear, to be replaced by a simple and uniform code of justice based on the common wants and interests of all men.[*] The connection between inequality of social conditions and what Tocqueville calls honor is a "close and necessary" one:

If it were allowable to suppose that all the races of mankind should be commingled, and that all the nations of earth should ultimately come to have the same interests and the same wants, undistinguished from each other by any characteristic peculiarities, no *conventional* value whatever would then be attached to men's actions; they would all be regarded by all in the same light. The general necessities of mankind, revealed by conscience to every man, would become the common standard. The only notions that would be recognized in the world would be the

---

majority is always thought to be right, without any moral power above it, while the second simply observes that "a completely democratic government is so dangerous an instrument that, *even in America,* men have been obliged to take a host of precautions against the errors and passions of Democracy" (Tocqueville, *Journey to America,* p. 149). In the *Democracy* itself, he argues that "a general law, which bears the name of justice, has been made and sanctioned not only by a majority of this or that people, but by a majority of mankind. The rights of every people are therefore confined within the limits of what is just.... When I refuse to obey an unjust law, I do not contest the right of the majority to command, but I simply appeal from the sovereignty of the people to the sovereignty of mankind" (*Democracy,* I, 269). Whatever the imprecision of this formulation, Tocqueville did not believe that any majority, even a majority of the whole of mankind, had a right to do whatever it pleased. The law that limits even this majority derives from the nature of man; deviations from it take the form of serving special interests. To be just, the majority must take its bearing from what is common to all.

[*] For a modern expression of this same theme, see, e.g., Fromm, *Man for Himself,* pp. 240–44.

simple and general ones of right and wrong, to which, by a natural and necessary tie, the ideas of approbation or censure would be attached.

Thus, to put all my meaning in a single proposition, the dissimilarities and inequalities of men gave rise to the notion of honor; that notion is weakened in proportion as these differences are obliterated, and with them it would disappear.[71]

As conditions become equal, conventional moral codes will wither away, to be succeeded by a natural morality corresponding to the natural condition of man. Democracy is the only social condition that does not give rise to a conventional code of morality, and in this democracy receives its justification: it alone is in accordance with nature.

The idea that the ground for the only legitimate moral code might be discovered in the general necessities of mankind was the basic premise of the exponents of natural rights, Hobbes and Locke, for example. There is, however, no thematic presentation of a doctrine of natural rights in Tocqueville, partly because that doctrine had already been discredited by Rousseau, partly because of Tocqueville's aversion to seventeenth-century philosophical abstractions. But he clearly does not altogether free himself from the idea of natural rights. For him, as for his predecessors in this tradition, the first and most fundamental natural right is individual liberty. As already noted, every man has by nature "an equal and indefeasible right . . . to regulate as he wishes his own destiny." In deference to the natural rights of all, men develop the concept of justice, of political virtue:

After the general idea of virtue, I know no higher principle than that of rights; these two ideas, rather, are united in one. The idea of rights is simply that of virtue introduced into the political world. It was the idea of rights that enabled men to define anarchy and tyranny, that taught them how to be independent without arrogance and to obey without servility. The man who submits to violence is debased by his compliance; but when he submits to a right of authority that he acknowledges in a fellow creature, he rises in some measure above the person who gives the command. There are no great men without virtue; and there are no great nations—it may almost be added, there would be no society—without respect for rights, for what is a union of rational and intelligent beings who are held together only by the bond of force? [p]

The history of the doctrine of natural rights does not seem to establish any necessary connection between natural rights and democracy. Certainly Hobbes thought that recognition of natural rights, and insistence on them, did not diminish either the legitimacy or the desirability of absolute monarchy. The more moderate Locke still did not argue that democracy was the only legitimate inference to be drawn from the concept of natural rights. Nevertheless, it may be shown that in the deepest sense democracy "has a certain privileged position within [this] framework,"[72] one that is tacitly acknowledged in the requirement that sovereignty can emerge only out of the unanimous consent of all who are a party to the contract. Tocqueville appears to have distilled from the doctrine of natural rights this single overpowering idea, and to have seen in it the only source of political legitimacy. In this sense we may grasp the profundity of Guizot's remark to Tocqueville: "You judge 'democracy' like an aristocrat who has been vanquished, and is convinced his conqueror is right."[73]

---

[p] Tocqueville, *Democracy*, I, 254. The translation has been corrected to preserve Tocqueville's emphasis on rights rather than right.

II

The Problem of Democracy

EVEN if democracy is the only just social condition, it need not coincide with a condition of human excellence; it is not necessarily conducive to what is highest in man. This observation, along with the tension implied by it between justice and excellence, forced Tocqueville to make a critical choice. Traditionally, justice had been considered equivalent to human excellence, or at least an expression of it. In a striking passage at the end of the *Democracy*, Tocqueville acquiesces to the modern separation of justice and excellence and accepts the priority of the claim of justice. "A state of equality is perhaps less elevated, but it is more just: and its justice constitutes its greatness and its beauty."[1] That justice and excellence should continue to be so separated, however, struck Tocqueville as lamentable, and his efforts were therefore directed toward reintegrating the two within the framework of modern democracy.

Yet this hardly conveys the poignancy of Tocqueville's concern with democracy. After all, a regime in which human greatness was by and large unknown but in which most men lived at a tolerably decent level of humanity might not be the cause of any great despair. But worse is possible. The last words of the *Democracy* warn that democracy may be accompanied by an unparalleled descent into servitude and barbarism. It is as if the realization of justice on earth and the simultaneous demise of civilization itself were compatible in thought. Bizarre conception!

Tocqueville is concerned to show that the triumph of

democracy, of equality of conditions, can and will result in the destruction of civilization unless certain countermeasures are instituted. If the trend toward barbarism is not stopped, man might eventually descend to a condition not far removed from that of the brutes. This possibility is remote, and perhaps not to be taken very seriously. But it is very likely that democratic man's primary concerns will be domestic ones, and that he will be isolated from those outside his family group by an obsession with the means of improving or sustaining his livelihood, by a narrowness of imagination, and by a kind of psychological anxiety that will replace the fear arising from physical dangers in a Hobbesian state of nature. Tocqueville also sees a more attractive side to his nature: when his own security is not at stake, democratic man displays a strong sense of compassion for his fellows. All things considered, Tocqueville's "democratic man," like Rousseau's "natural man," is a sort of prepolitical atavist. What democracy most jeopardizes are the virtues closely associated with a political order: not only patriotism, the habit of acting on what is good for the whole rather than for the individual, but also civil or rational freedom, the ability and the opportunity to participate in the formulation of public policy. The disappearance of patriotism foreshadows the disappearance of the possibility of greatness, for in Tocqueville's vocabulary greatness involves power exercised on a grand scale, with consequences of an enduring character. Elements of greatness might be seen in the restless, energetic activity that so captivated Tocqueville in America, but if the energy of the Americans were to be directed to the commercial rather than the political arena, as Tocqueville predicted it would, the active American scene might appear more as a conglomeration of petty actions initiated by those with petty desires.[a]

[a] The promotion of legislation designed to stimulate such energy had been part of the deliberate intention of Hamilton in 1791. In his *Report on Manufac-*

Tocqueville's understanding of democratic man may be based largely on Rousseau, but his portrayal of democratic man was drawn from his study of America. Hence, a study of Tocqueville must inquire into the intellectual significance for him of his visit to America.[b] According to his lifelong friend Gustave de Beaumont, the questions that appear to have arisen as a result of the visit to America were actually present in Tocqueville's mind before it:

The great problems, which were to be the business of his life, which he would one day go to a new world to study, already rose to his mind. How to reconcile equality, which separates and isolates men, with liberty? How to prevent a power, the offspring of democracy, from becoming absolute and tyrannical? Where to find a force able to contend against this power among a set of men all equal, it is true, but all equally weak and impotent? Was the fate of modern society to be both democracy and despotism?[2]

Tocqueville's choice of America as a model reflected his belief that America had solved many of the problems of democracy that still occupied France at the time. When he begins his work on the old regime and the French Revolution, it is as a physician addressing a patient whose prognosis is uncertain.[3] France is sick; America is healthy. It is not only that France had not recovered from the effects of her revolution: as Tocqueville was fond of repeating, the end of her revolution was not yet in sight.

Instead of looking to Rousseau for the principles of their regime, as the French did, the Americans looked to the

---

tures he had written, "Even things in themselves not positively advantageous sometimes become so by their tendency to provoke exertion. Every new scene which is opened to the busy nature of man to rouse and exert itself is the addition of a new energy to the general stock of effort." (Hamilton, IV, 94.) Tocqueville would no doubt have argued that such legislation only encouraged or elicited what was latent in the democratic spirit itself.

[b] The visit, as Pierson has pointed out (pp. 12ff), had political significance as well: it was a handy escape from certain embarrassments following the July Revolution of 1830.

good doctor Locke and his common-sense commercialism. Tocqueville is like Rousseau in his concern with virtue and citizenship, believing with him that these are the characteristics most likely to be lost in contemporary society. Hence, perhaps paradoxically, the appropriateness of America as a model. It was not that the Americans were vice-ridden, or irreligious, or unpatriotic, for by and large they were not; but the cultivation or inducement of virtue was not the function of their regime, and in this respect America was a model of a *modern* democracy. Other regimes, most notably that of the French during the Revolution, had not divested themselves of the impulse toward moral reformation. It is in this sense that Tocqueville could describe America as "the image of democracy itself."[4]

Concomitant with the explicit contrast in Tocqueville's writings between modern democracy and feudal aristocracy is a less explicit but by no means insignificant contrast between ancient and modern democracy. Tocqueville completely rejects the relevance to modern problems of classical political experience, particularly that of the democracies of antiquity:

> When I compare the Greek and Roman Republics with these American states; the manuscript libraries of the former, and their rude population, with the innumerable journals and the enlightened people of the latter; when I remember all the attempts that are made to judge the modern republics by the aid of those of antiquity, and to infer what will happen in our time from what took place two thousand years ago, I am tempted to burn my books in order to apply none but novel ideas to so novel a condition of society.[5]

What is it that warrants his rejection? To begin with, there is the alleged irrelevance of the political experience of small city-states. Most of the literature up to the modern era had maintained that a decent democracy (i.e., one compatible with virtue) was possible only within the confines of a small area. But in the modern era this limitation was overcome through the mechanism of representation—a major breakthrough. Tocqueville, in his address on Cherbuliez's "Democracy in Switzerland," sounded the death knell of the small state organized as a pure democracy: "The pure democracies of Switzerland belong to another age; they can teach nothing about the present or the future. . . . Each century has its dominating spirit which nothing can resist. . . . One must consider the small governments of the Swiss cantons as the last and respectable debris of a world that is no longer."*c*

The representative principle, Tocqueville suggests, might work to mitigate evils traditionally associated with democracy. For example, he rejects the hypothesis that the citizenry of democratic regimes will experience volatile changes in their opinions and feelings. He remarks that this hypothesis "may be true of small democratic nations, like those of the ancient world, in which the whole community could be assembled in a public place and then excited at will by an orator," but he finds no evidence that the hypothesis may be applicable to America.[6] Behind the apparent mobility of opinion in America, in fact, is a remarkable and even depressing stability of opinions about religion, morality, and politics; the mobility itself extends only to details, or to new consequences flowing from old convictions.

Nevertheless, the importance of size (and correspondingly, of the principle of representation) can be exaggerated. If representatives are but little better than their con-

---

c Tocqueville, *Oeuvres Complètes* (Mayer), I, Part 2, 356. No less a figure than John Stuart Mill acknowledged his indebtedness to Tocqueville for having first demonstrated to him the impossibility of a pure democracy in the modern age. (Mill, *Autobiography*, pp. 161–62.)

stituents, the hoped-for improvement in the government of democracies may come almost to naught. Tocqueville warns that "it may well be believed that in the end the delegate will conform to the principles of his constituents and favor their propensities as much as their interests."[7] Without discounting entirely the significance of the representative system, we may affirm that its development was not responsible for the alleged superiority of modern over classical democracy, nor for reducing the classical experience to a matter of merely antiquarian interest.

Of Tocqueville's belief in the superiority of modern democracy there is little question. In his disparagement of classical democracy he goes so far as to deny even the applicability of the term "democracy" to the ancient republics, Athens in particular.

What was called the People in the most democratic republics of antiquity was very unlike what we designate by that term. In Athens all the citizens took part in public affairs; but there were only twenty thousand citizens to more than three hundred and fifty thousand inhabitants. All the rest were slaves, and discharged the greater part of those duties which belong at the present day to the lower or even to the middle classes. Athens, then, with her universal suffrage, was, after all, merely an aristocratic republic, in which all the nobles had an equal right to the government.[d]

It is the institution of slavery then, that distinguishes ancient democracy from modern. "[The] different effects of slavery

---

[d] Tocqueville, *Democracy*, II, 65. In his rejection of the relevance of classical democracy, Tocqueville anticipated the work of Fustel de Coulanges, who less than a decade after Tocqueville's death was to make the same point in his own classic, *The Ancient City* (p. 11): "Having imperfectly observed the institutions of the ancient city, men have dreamed of reviving them among us. They have deceived themselves about the liberty of the ancients, and on this very account liberty among the moderns has been put in peril. The last eighty years have

and freedom may readily be understood; and they suffice to explain many of the differences which we notice between the civilization of antiquity and that of our own time."[8] A civilization in which only a few are free can offer no guidance to one in which all are. Classical democracy had not understood the principle of freedom. "The most profound and capacious minds of Rome and Greece were never able to reach the idea, at once so general and so simple, of the common likeness of men and of the common birthright of each to freedom [*du droit égal que chacun d'eux apporte, en naissant, à la liberté*]; they tried to prove that slavery was in the order of nature and that it would always exist." Tocqueville attributes the acceptance of the idea of the natural equality of all men as originating in the teachings of Christ.[9] Curiously, despite Christianity's triumph, until the modern age no republic had been erected on a foundation of natural rights. This development could not occur until the political implication of the idea of equality—that every man must enjoy the right of participation in his government—was understood. Tocqueville recognizes that this enlargement of the original concept is "wholly modern" and that "it alone is sufficient to constitute a great difference between our times and all that has preceded."[10] Thus, what is new in modern times is the recognition of the right of all to citizenship; in America, this idea of the sovereignty of all has been most nearly realized. It was in America, Tocqueville says, looking back, that "the great experiment of the attempt to construct society upon a new basis was to be made by civilized man; and it was there, for the first time, that theories hitherto unknown, or deemed impracticable, were to exhibit a spectacle

---

clearly shown that one of the great difficulties which impede the march of modern society is the habit which it has of always keeping Greek and Roman antiquity before its eyes."

for which the world had not been prepared by the history of the past."[11] America is thus the regime in which the consequences of the idea of equality, among them the equal participation of all in the processes of government, may best be studied.

"Another point demonstrated by America is that virtue is not, as it has long been pretended, the only thing which can preserve Republics, but that enlightenment *more than anything else* facilitates that social state. The Americans are hardly more virtuous than others, but they are infinitely better educated (I speak of the mass) than any other people of my acquaintance."[e]

We may say, then, that in Tocqueville's view great progress has occurred since classical times. Classical democracy was deficient in its failure to understand the principle of freedom, in its misjudgment of the possibilities latent in a reliance upon self-interest, and in its Periclean insistence on the paramount role of virtue. In modern times, the Christian concept of the equality of all men has been adopted as the foundation of government, and in education of a particular kind a substitute has been found for the classical training in virtue.

Despite the apparent irrelevance of classical democracy, Tocqueville points out one respect in which its success reproaches the modern world. Classical democracy had been characterized by public-spiritedness, while in the modern world individualism has eroded the justification for devoting oneself to the public realm. According to Tocqueville, patriotism was "the passion that constituted the life of the nations of antiquity."[12]

---

[e] Tocqueville, *Journey to America*, p. 258 (italics mine). The enlightment of which Tocqueville speaks refers to the practice by Americans of the doctrine of self-interest rightly understood. Cf. Aron, pp. 177–78: "Ancient republics were egalitarian, but virtuous. . . . Modern democracy, as seen by Tocqueville, is fundamentally a commercial and industrial society. . . . One can therefore say that the principle . . . of modern democracy . . . is self-interest, and not virtue."

Till I reflected upon the present behavior of our armies, I thought that there was much exaggeration in the accounts handed down to us of the public virtues of the ancients. I could not understand how the men of those days were capable of them. For, after all, man is the same in every age. The every-day conduct of our armies explains the mystery. Civil society was at that time constituted as military society is now. The men of those days, as individuals, were not better than we are; in private life they were probably worse. But in public life they were subjected to an organization, a discipline, a prevailing opinion; to fixed customs and traditions, which forced them to a conduct different from ours.[13]

The everyday conduct of armies, as Tocqueville makes clear in the letter just quoted, results not from respect for equal rights, but from the imposition and acceptance of obligations and duties. In altering the basis of the franchise for participation in public life from virtue or duty to rights, modern democracy has damped the forces that make patriotism flourish. Not only does the doctrine of natural rights tend to weaken the traditional forces of social cohesion; it also subjects the state to the onerous task of justifying, to an unprecedented degree, the demands it typically makes of its citizenry. This is the first intimation we have that the progress from classical to modern times has been accompanied by consequences that may make it equivocal.

The problematic character of this progress is indicated also by the responsibility Christianity itself apparently bears for its part in undermining the spirit of patriotism. Contrasting pagan religion with Christianity, Tocqueville notes:

The pagan religions of antiquity were always more or less linked up with the political institutions and the social order of their environment, and their dogmas were conditioned to some extent by the interests of the nations, or even the cities, where they flourished. A pagan religion functioned within the limits of a given country and rarely spread beyond its frontiers. . . .

Christianity, however, made light of all the barriers which had prevented the pagan religions from spreading ... and partly owed its triumph to the fact that, far more than any other religion, it was catholic in the exact sense, having no links with any specific form of government, social order, period, or nation.*

The civil support that the republics of antiquity received from parochial religions is denied modern republics, for the doctrine of their religion transcends national boundaries. In practice, this ultimate implication of Christianity has more often than not been tempered by injunctions to render unto Caesar his due. Moreover, it might be argued that the effectiveness of Christian doctrine in weakening the ties of public virtue could not be fully experienced until the concept of the equality of all men had been given a this-worldly orientation, and that for this reorientation Christianity itself could not be held responsible. Yet the tension created by the demands of Christianity on the one hand and those of patriotism on the other becomes one of Tocqueville's principal concerns. "The organization and establishment of democracy *in Christendom*," he had written in the *Democracy*, "is the great political problem of our times."[14]

---

*Tocqueville, *Old Régime*, p. 12. Cf. Tocqueville's letter to Mme. Swetchine of October 20, 1856: "Without doubt, Christianity can exist under every government. This is an evidence of its truth. It never has been bound, and never will be bound, to any form of government, or to the grandeur of any single nation." (*Memoir*, II, 333.) On the question of the relationship of Christianity to the decline in public virtue, Tocqueville wrote to Prince Albert de Broglie: "How is it that the Christian religion, which has in so many respects improved individuals and advanced our race, has exercised, especially in the beginning, so little influence over the progress of society? Why is it that in proportion as men become more humane, more just, more temperate, more chaste, they seem everyday more and more indifferent to public virtue; so much so that the great family of the nation seems more corrupt, more base, and more tottering while every little individual family is better regulated? ... This contrast ... between Christian virtues and what I call public virtue, has frequently reappeared. There is nothing which seems to me so difficult of explanation, when we consider that God, and after Him his revelation, are the foundations, or rather the sources, of all virtues, the practice of which is necessary in the different states of mankind." (Letter of July 20, 1856, *Memoir*, II, 317.)

Investigating Tocqueville's turn to America has disclosed, I believe, that he conceives political life in our time as being composed of elements that have undergone radical transformation since their ancient inception. He confronts feudal aristocracy with democracy on the basis of a rejection of classical democracy, a rejection made in the name of freedom, natural rights, and Christianity. The paganism of antiquity has been replaced by Christianity, and the sovereignty of the few by the natural sovereignty of all. But the public-spiritedness of antiquity has been succeeded by the self-interest and individual concern of the modern age, and the spirit of enlightenment has taken the role once filled by virtue. Modern democracy is not, after all, unequivocally superior to its classical predecessor. Almost all the problems Tocqueville confronts—equality, freedom, self-interest, virtue, patriotism, and religion—have their counterpart in the classical experience, an experience that does not provide any clear solution. The locus of these problems in the modern world was America. America was the archetype of a Christian democracy, a democracy of a wholly new kind.

Tocqueville's turn to America also reflects a methodological commitment. His approach to the study of politics departs from the method of the writers of the seventeenth and eighteenth centuries who began their inquiries with the study of man simply (for example, man in the state of nature), irrespective of his citizenship in a given regime. Tocqueville, like Burke before him, avoids the abstractness of the philosophers of the Enlightenment and embraces instead the concrete, the political. This does not prevent him from generalizing about the nature of man and the human condition, but his generalizations appear to derive from his research into a particular, actual, human situation.

His study of politics begins with an inquiry into one facet of that human situation, namely, social condition:

Social condition is commonly the result of circumstances, sometimes of laws, oftener still of these two causes united; but when once established, it may justly be considered as itself the source of almost all the laws, the usages, and the ideas which regulate the conduct of nations: whatever it does not produce, it modifies. If we would become acquainted with the legislation and the manners of a nation, therefore, we must begin by the study of its social condition.[15]

The two volumes of *Democracy in America* are explicitly devoted to an exposition of the way in which a particular social condition has made itself felt, both in the political institutions of America and in the customs, manners, and intellectual habits of its citizens. Social condition is the appropriate focus of attention, according to Tocqueville, not only because it is the condition that characterizes the regime, but also because (in classical terminology) it is the principle that sets the regime in motion. In a fundamental sense, it is the cause of a regime's having its own particular characteristics. This is not to say that social condition explains everything about a society: antecedent customs, geographical factors, and the like also shape the regime. But these secondary factors will never conceal or frustrate the operation of the fundamental moving principle for long. Social condition forms opinions and modifies passions and feelings; it determines the goals pursued, the type of man admired, the language in use, and, ultimately, the character of the men who live under it.

Tocqueville's comprehensive analysis of the way in which the principle of a regime impresses itself on every aspect of life under that regime—so that the differences between regimes can be stated in terms of the differences in their principles—is classical in its approach. In his mode of analysis, at least, Tocqueville, following Montesquieu, returns to classical models. Tocqueville's indebtedness to Montesquieu

in this respect does not prevent him from taking exception
to certain views he associates with Montesquieu: he denies,
for example, that nations "obey some insurmountable and
unintelligent power, arising from anterior events—from
their race, or from the soil and climate of their country."[16]
But he shares with Montesquieu, as well as with Plato and
Aristotle, the view that the springs that set regimes in motion—honor, courage, wisdom, fear, equality—may be said
to be their causes. It is true that for all practical purposes
Tocqueville considers only two such principles, equality and
inequality; but he looks on equality and inequality as the
extremes of the spectrum of social and political principles
that motivate every regime. His works are thus intended
to convey his reflections about political things as such, not
merely his understanding of democracy. In point of fact, of
course, it is through his awareness of aristocracy as the ultimate political alternative that he is able to take the measure
of democracy itself.

Two obstacles apparently stand in the way of our coming
to grips immediately with Tocqueville's understanding of
democracy. In the first place, Tocqueville has been roundly
criticized not only for equating democracy with equality of
conditions, that is, for confusing an idea with a social fact,
but even more so for using the term democracy imprecise-
ly throughout *Democracy in America*.[9] This is startling:
Tocqueville himself (in the very same work) inveighs
against those who use a word ambiguously, and dreads that
"the meaning of a word in our own language should become
indeterminate."[17] It would be surprising if he were to fail
to apply these standards to the most important term he uses.
He could be precise about the meaning of democracy, as is

[9] Pierson, for example (pp. 104, 451, 459), counts seven or eight different
senses in which it is used. There is an excellent discussion of this point in Lively,
pp. 49–50; see also the essay by Phillips Bradley in *Democracy*, II, 407–8.

demonstrated in his notes for the final volume of the *European Revolution*:

We . . . live in an inextricable confusion of ideas, to the great advantage of demagogues and of despots. . . . [Democracy] can mean only one thing in the true sense . . . a government where the people more or less participate in their government. Its sense is intimately bound to the idea of political liberty. To give the democratic epithet to a government where there is no political liberty is a palpable absurdity, since this departs from the natural meaning of these words.[18]

But in the *Democracy* Tocqueville does precisely what he here condemns: he speaks of democratic liberty as well as of democratic tyranny. Yet before we conclude that such inconsistency can only be understood as a serious lapse on his part, we would do well to consider his purpose in the *Democracy*: to show men how they may be *both* equal *and* free. The danger was that men might achieve equality at the price of freedom. By not making democracy synonymous with any institutional form associated with it, by not restricting the range of its meaning to the political arena (government of the people, representative government, separation of powers) Tocqueville underscored his fear that democracy as most men understood it—namely, participation by the many in the act of sovereignty—was compatible with tyranny as well as with liberty. More precisely, tyranny could coexist with what appeared to be democratic institutions. A regime could not be understood solely in terms of its political foundations. Unlike some of his contemporaries, who believed that the gradual development of equality meant the gradual but final destruction of the possibility of tyranny on earth, Tocqueville understood that the democratic principle could lead to a despotism never before experienced.

The second obstacle has to do with the criticism of those

who despair at the carelessness with which Tocqueville tends to confuse and confound democratic things with things peculiarly American. Bryce, for example, asserts that in practice Tocqueville "underrates the purely local and special features of America, and often ... treats it as a norm for democracy in general."[19] That Tocqueville is not unmindful of this difficulty is indicated by his repeated warnings not to confuse democracy with American practice, and it is with his warning in mind that we must approach *Democracy in America*. To take an obvious example, equality of conditions had not determined the geographical setting of the United States, but the Americans' disposition to deal with their physical environment in one way rather than in another *was* in large measure determined by the character they had acquired through the operation of equality of conditions. A people in whom the acquisitive instinct had been unleashed by the democratic principle would and did regard the gifts of nature in a different manner than would their neighbors living under different regimes.[20]

Unfortunately, Tocqueville's awareness of the need to distinguish democratic things from American things as such does not relieve the reader of the responsibility for making this distinction himself. Tocqueville devotes one chapter in the *Democracy* to problems, such as relations between the races in the United States, that are specifically "American without being democratic."[21] In this chapter he characterizes as "American" certain attitudes—such as the emphasis on self-interest, natural rights, continual change, and perfectibility—that he either has or will subsequently (in the second volume) come to identify with the nature of democracy itself.[22]

Three conclusions about his procedure seem warranted. First, that he fails, in part, to make proper distinctions. Second, that acknowledging this much we may nevertheless agree with Lively that Tocqueville's concern with American things was wholly subordinate to his concern with democracy.[23] (Hence, insofar as I am explicating Tocqueville, I shall deal primarily with the latter concern.) Third, that so forewarned, we should not be surprised to find very pregnant material for an understanding of democracy itself in his discussions of matters that are put forward as American only, as in the case of the chapter on race relations.

We are, perhaps, too prone to accept it as a matter of course that equality (and ultimately equality of conditions) should be the principle of democracy. The demands for equality in the civil rights struggle of the Fifties and Sixties seem to confirm our own identification of democracy with certain conceptions of equality. And yet it has not always been so. We have only to go back to Montesquieu, to whom Tocqueville is explicitly indebted, to find the proposition that the principle of democracy is virtue, or a kind of public-spiritedness—although even Montesquieu regards approximate economic equality as indispensable to any democracy. The classical objections to democracy arose from the belief that democratic aspirations based on claims of equality diminished the likelihood of a regime of virtue, understood either as patriotism or as any other form of excellence. It is interesting to note that Aristotle, whom Tocqueville found "too antiquated" for his taste, came very close to Tocqueville's conception of democracy.[24] "The underlying idea of the democratic type of constitution," Aristotle tells us, "is liberty." This liberty has two facets—one political, one social—which derive from the concept of equality. On the political side, each citizen, whatever his merit and however firm his devotion to the common good, must count as one, and each must rule and be ruled in turn. On the social side, each citizen must be allowed to live as he sees fit—a demand Aristotle recognizes as the ideal of "freedom from any interference of government." Should the ideal fail—should freedom *from* government as well as freedom from any responsibility *for* government prove unattainable —then, Aristotle says, democratic men will settle for nothing less than "such freedom as comes from the interchange of ruling and being ruled."[25] They will not permit a settled, fixed order of rule. Inevitably, the distinction between those who care for the common good and those who do not would be rejected as an improper criterion for use in selecting men for high office; freedom (or equality) would be completely divorced from virtue. The end would be national disaster.

Intended or not, this description is surely a caricature of any actual democratic regime. Selection by lot may be resorted to in trivial matters, but no regime could survive if the principle of equality were not mitigated at some point and in some way by the claims of virtue. Montesquieu's identification of the democratic principle with virtue may thus be understood as the minimum precondition for turning democracy into a viable regime. But Montesquieu had also discovered that at least one contemporary quasi-popular regime had found in the pursuit of self-centered acquisitive goals a modern substitute for virtue. The full growth of the commercial spirit in England had made possible a regime that was not only viable, but in which the arts and sciences flourished.[26] Tocqueville and Montesquieu may have differed over whether England or America was the better example of a regime in which self-interest took the place of virtue, but they agree completely that the modern world made it possible to gain an entirely new understanding of democracy. The discovery of a substitute for virtue, moreover, had the effect of unshackling equality: freed from the restraints traditionally imposed on it, equality makes its appearance, perhaps for the first time, with an unabashed claim to be the sole principle of democracy. Few have captured the sense of Tocqueville's conception of equality as well as Faguet:

Tocqueville never defined Democracy, but he made it everywhere apparent what he meant by the word. To him it is the need which man feels, not by any means to suppress government, but to suppress hierarchy. What annoys man is not the fact of being governed but of being dominated, so to speak, menaced; not of having to obey but of having to respect; not of being restrained but of having to bow down; not of being a slave but of being inferior. This sentiment is neither good nor bad; it is natural and it is eternal.[27]

In emphasizing equality of conditions rather than equality per se, Tocqueville not only reveals his methodological revulsion from certain types of abstractions, but makes a more important point, by calling attention to a state of society in which the concept of equality has been put into practice. It is a state of society in which men confront each other when their equality has been lifted from the pages of the philosophers and made real to them in equal opportunities for education, in a general leveling of wealth, in equality before the law, and in the uniform assurance of political rights. Above all, it is a state of society characterized by the absence of permanent hierarchical arrangements, whether political, social, or economic. Obviously, such a state does not preclude the formation of distinctions between men based on differences of wealth, education, or the like; but in principle at least, and to a remarkable degree in practice, each man in such a society counts equally. Tocqueville did not regard America, or any regime, as one in which the principle of equality had been fully put into practice, but America approximated this condition for him more than any other regime. In one of his notebooks, he summarized the state of things as he viewed them:

Men in America, as with us, are ranked according to certain categories by the give and take of social life: common habits, education, and especially wealth establish these classifications; but these rules are neither absolute, nor inflexible, nor permanent. They establish passing distinctions and by no means form classes properly so called; they give no superiority, even in thought, to one man over another. So that although two men may never see each other in the same drawing-rooms, if they meet outside, they meet without pride on one side or envy on the other. At bottom they feel themselves to be, and they are, equal.[28]

Tocqueville's observations on democratic society have been reproduced, summarized, criticized, and made the object of further research and inquiry down to the present day. Their own fame, together with the profusion of secondary materials, renders unnecessary any detailed recounting of all his insights into the ways of democracy. The primary features need to be set forth; the individual ramifications must be passed over. However loath one may be, for example, to suppress Tocqueville's judgment that the education of women in a democracy may make them "cold and virtuous" instead of "affectionate wives and agreeable companions," one cannot very well equate this with his reflections on, say, the tyranny of the majority.[29]

The characteristic feature of democratic society is its atomism. Gone are the carefully prescribed codes, predominantly legal and contractual, that governed relations between the three classes of society in aristocratic times. Gone are the economic and social barriers that kept those classes distinct, but gone also is the sense of cohesiveness and responsibility that made aristocratic society an organic whole. "Aristocracy," Tocqueville tells us, "made a chain of all the members of the community, from the peasant to the king; democracy breaks that chain and severs every link of it."[30] The citizens of a democratic society have no natural ties to one another; each being the equal of every other, no one is obliged to be responsive to the needs or commands of another; nor is he, typically, except when his own interests are at stake. Each citizen preserves a sense of his own separateness, independence, and equality. He is, one might say, the center of a tiny private universe consisting of himself and his immediate circle of family and friends. Wholly absorbed in this universe, he loses sight of that greater universe, society at large.

According to Tocqueville, the cause of the atomism of democratic ages lies in the spread of "individualism," which he defines as a disposition to reject the legitimacy of any obligation or article of faith that has not been submitted to personal inquiry. The word, Tocqueville reminds us, is of recent origin; it is a word "to which a novel idea has given birth." Since its roots are intellectual, it must be distinguished from selfishness, the exaggerated love of self that originates "in blind instinct."[31] Selfishness is coeval with man; individualism can be traced to a philosophic doctrine arising at a specific time and place. The spiritual father of individualism is Descartes, whose philosophic method supplies the example and the justification for submitting all theories and beliefs to private judgment. In his chapter on the philosophic method of the Americans, Tocqueville describes a revolution of the mind whose consequences parallel those of the overthrow of feudalism:

In the sixteenth century reformers subjected some of the dogmas of the ancient faith to the scrutiny of private judgment; but they still withheld it from the discussion of all the rest. In the seventeenth century Bacon in the natural sciences and Descartes in philosophy properly so called abolished received formulas, destroyed the empire of tradition, and overthrew the authority of the schools. The philosophers of the eighteenth century, generalizing at length on the same principle, undertook to submit to the private judgment of each man all the objects of his belief.[32]

Descartes, though he had chosen to apply his method only to certain matters, "had made it fit to be applied to all."

What is the relation between individualism and equality of conditions? Which is cause, and which effect? Actually, they are not related causally. Whatever the ultimate causes of each, in democratic ages they complement each other. Democratic conditions encourage every man to seek within himself for an understanding of the world about him. The traditional sources of such an understanding—custom, one's superiors, one's forefathers, one's social class, even the inherited wisdom of religion or philosophy—have all lost their aura of authority. There is little choice but to fall back on one's own resources. Equality of conditions is thus responsible for the ready and widespread acceptance of individualism, and individualism is a welcome ally of democracy in its attempts to overturn the social and political restraints of the Middle Ages.[h]

Tocqueville's attitude toward the new doctrine appears to be straightforwardly negative: "Individualism proceeds from erroneous judgment ... it originates as much in deficiencies of mind as in perversity of heart."[33] This is readily accounted for by his fear that excessive enthusiasm for individualism may carry societies to the brink of dissolution. A sense of community is built upon tradition and custom, whose strength is directly proportional to the degree to which they are *not* subjected to individual inquiry. America, for example, has been spared the effects of extreme individualism by the fortuitous persistence of religious beliefs that act to unite the nation and to confine speculation within salutary limits.

Still, no liberal (and Tocqueville considers himself one) could possibly be altogether critical of individualism. In fact, Tocqueville goes to great lengths to defend and en-

[h] See below, pp. 138–39.

courage the positive results of the new spirit of inquiry and independence. Another unfortunate thing about individualism, however, is that it seems to generate a kind of dialectic of its own, which, when it has proceeded to its conclusion, eventuates in authoritarianism. Though this authoritarianism is surely different in origin and character from that against which individualism originally rebelled, it is a form of authoritarianism nonetheless.

> . . . I perceive how, under the dominion of certain laws, democracy would extinguish that liberty of the mind to which a democratic social condition is favorable; so that, after having broken all the bondage once imposed on it by ranks or by men, the human mind would be closely fettered to the general will of the greatest number.
>
> If the absolute power of a majority were to be substituted by democratic nations for all the different powers that checked or retarded overmuch the energy of individual minds, the evil would only have changed character. . . . For myself, when I feel the hand of power lie heavy on my brow, I care but little to know who oppresses me. . . .[34]

Thus, if democracy is to survive, or if it is to fulfill the expectations that may be held of it, individualism as a social force must have its anti-societal tendencies neutralized (it must cease to act as the solvent of society), and society in turn must be rendered incapable of destroying the independence that individualism fosters. Individualism must be weakened or transformed, but not made impotent. What is needed is a salutary individualism.

In his *Discourse on the Origin of Inequality,* Rousseau had observed that the love of well-being, the desire for the material comforts that make life something more than a struggle for mere subsistence, was the exclusive motive of human behavior.[35] Tocqueville is less concerned with ascertaining whether it is man's prime desire than he is with describing the special force it takes on when linked with individualism and equality of conditions. It is, he admits, a "natural and instinctive" desire; as such, it is more or less present in every man, but in most men it lives a kind of marginal existence until a social condition arises that allows it to assert itself to the fullest. Equality of conditions renders the passion for well-being "peculiarly intense," infuses it into "the heart of every man," and makes it "the prominent and indelible feature of democratic times."[36] If equality of conditions is accompanied, as indeed it is, by skepticism about eventual heavenly rewards, it is only logical that most men should become attached "to the only prospects that remain before them, to the benefits of this world."[37]

The liberation of the drive for well-being has far-reaching political and social consequences. Under the conditions of the old regime, the disparity of wealth and well-being had been accepted as part of the natural order of things. The few who had had the opportunity as well as the right to enjoy creature comforts had managed to satisfy their desires in a way that also left them free to develop other pursuits. Confident that the wealth they enjoyed would not at any moment be seized from them, the nobility could, for example, turn their attention to studies in the arts and sciences, as well as to the tasks of government. With the overthrow of the feudal system and the advent of individualism, well-being was seen as a natural right of *all* men. Democracy, then, must satisfy the desire for well-being not of a few, but of all; but unless it is prepared to abandon the communal and cultural achievements that elevate men, it must fulfill this demand in a way that will induce some men, at least, to devote a part of their energies to other concerns.

Taking a cue from feudal times, we might see a solution if material goods could be produced to the extent that no one need fear getting a smaller share than he desired, or if democratic man could learn to moderate his desires. Even so, we would still have to assume that with the acquisition of his share a man would typically turn his attention to other matters. Tocqueville appears to hold two conflicting views on the likelihood of solving the problem. At first, he seems confident that the search for physical gratification will be kept within modest bounds. Democratic man is not one to build sumptuous monuments to his sensuality, to wear out his life in continual acts of depravity. His is rather a simple search for the little comforts of life: to acquire the means to render life less arduous, perhaps to purchase and plant a few more acres of land, or to enlarge his dwelling. "In democratic society the sensuality of the public has taken a moderate and tranquil course . . . ." Tocqueville's reproach to the principle of equality is not that it encourages men to pursue criminal gratifications, "but that it absorbs them wholly in quest of those that are allowed. By these means a kind of honest materialism may ultimately be established in the world, [a materialism] that would not corrupt, but enervate the soul, and noiselessly unbend its springs of action." The sudden, dramatic and violent rejection of religion, morality, and property that had erupted in 1789 was but a temporary attitude, characteristic only of a revolutionary period; it should not be thought of as a permanent characteristic of democratic eras. Democratic man's desire for well-being is not only compatible with morality and public order, but may even require them. It may even be combined with "a species of religious morality." Nevertheless, Tocqueville is apprehensive lest in the pursuit of well-being democratic men "lose sight of those more precious possessions that constitute the glory and the greatness of mankind."[38]

Although democracy thus may be accompanied by the neglect of what is highest in man, at least it will provide a modest well-being for the greatest number. This is the virtue Tocqueville celebrates in his famous conclusion to the second part of the *Democracy*. But an insatiable thirst for even modest comforts may generate great economic problems: where will the goods come from? Moreover, Tocqueville's account of the characteristic restraint with which democratic man exercises his taste for well-being ("to add a few yards of land to your field, to plant an orchard, to enlarge a dwelling, to be always making life more comfortable and convenient, to avoid trouble . . .")[39] is in striking contrast with the image of democratic man in America given just a few pages later:

In the United States a man builds a house in which to spend his old age, and he sells it before the roof is on; he plants a garden and lets it just as the trees are coming into bearing; he brings a field into tillage and leaves other men to gather the crops; he embraces a profession and gives it up; he settles in a place, which he soon afterwards leaves to carry his changeable longings elsewhere. . . . Death at length overtakes him, but it is before he is weary of his bootless chase of that complete felicity which forever escapes him.[40]

The second account more accurately depicts Tocqueville's view of what occurs when all avenues to the satisfaction of the desire for well-being are opened, but opened equally to all. The competition is terrific. However much a man may have, he thinks continually of the vast store of goods that constantly eludes him, a thought that "fills him with anxiety, fear, and regret, and keeps his mind in ceaseless trepidation."[41] A materialistic hedonism thus can only bring unhappiness, not pleasure; in turn, there can be no technological solution to the problem of well-being. The desires of men increase as they are gratified; there can never be enough for all.

This unexpected shift from a virtuous or decent materialism to a more or less thoroughgoing hedonism results from the rise of the commercial spirit—commerce being seen as the most effective means of satisfying the taste for well-being. Commerce readily transforms the simple desire for modest comforts into a caricature of its former self. Commerce and manufacture not only intensify the desire for well-being, but impart a peculiar tone to the whole society:

All men who live in democratic times more or less contract the ways of thinking of the manufacturing and trading classes; their minds take a serious, deliberate, and positive turn; they are apt to relinquish the ideal in order to pursue some visible and proximate object which appears to be the natural and necessary aim of their desires. Thus the principle of equality does not destroy the imagination, but lowers its flight to the level of earth.[42]

Commerce comes to be regarded as the noblest of all pursuits, and beguiles the faculties of the most able men in society. It offers for their exertions a grander and more challenging theater than politics. Men of superior intellect are thus diverted from politics to business, from public life to private affairs, there finding not only grand opportunities, but freedom from the conformity and vulgarity of political life as well. But even more is at stake than the loss of the ablest minds from public service. In a democratic society each man habitually thinks of himself and his family only; when, if ever, he thinks of the nation, it is solely as an instrument for the protection of his quest for material gain. The spirit of commerce even makes him regard all society as an oversize commercial enterprise, to be conducted along the same lines and in accordance with the same exclusive concern for gain as any other business. Politics becomes indistinguishable from commerce.[43]

Individualism and materialism, the divisive features of democracy, are offset to a degree by a general softening of manners and the growth of a spirit of compassion or human fellow-feeling. The manners, pursuits, and tastes of the classes of the Middle Ages were so different that they looked on each other as different species. Medieval society was cool, uncompromising, and severe. Men fulfilled duties that originated not in any natural obligation, but in a purely conventional code obligatory on noble and serf alike (*"pas du droit natural, mais du droit politique"*). "The claim of social duty was more stringent than that of mere humanity."[44] The democratic revolution, on the other hand, succeeds in dissolving social or political obligations while bringing natural human ties to the fore. As conditions become equal, men realize their essential similarity; this awareness evokes genuine empathy, and a simple act of the imagination suffices to enable one to experience the sufferings of another. There is, moreover, a direct link between the consequences of individualism and the growth of compassion. Contrary to what might have been expected, emancipation from traditional restraints does not leave democratic man confident in himself and proud of his new-found freedom. Confronted as he is on all sides by those who, like himself, are restlessly striving for unattainable goods, each citizen "is habitually engaged in the contemplation of a very puny object: namely, himself."[45] His demeanor is characteristically grave, filled as he is with "anxiety, fear, and regret." In the circumstances, he has no alternative but to seek the assistance of others, something he is more obliged to do the more equal social conditions become. However, although a condition of equality supports the increase of human fellow-feeling, this increase is limited by the inevitable conflict between each man's self-interest and his concern for others. In what amounts to a restatement of Rousseau's doctrine that man is naturally good, Tocqueville describes the role of compassion in democratic times: "In democratic ages men rarely sacrifice themselves for one another, but they display general compassion for the members of the human race. They inflict no useless ills, and they are happy to relieve the griefs of others when they can do so without much hurting themselves; they are not disinterested, but they are humane."[46]

It might appear that compassion and self-interest together could serve as the foundation of a social or political bond in democratic times, thus overcoming the divisive forces of individualism and materialism. But compassion and self-interest, though not necessarily opposed, are also not always compatible. Tocqueville, again like Rousseau, sees compassion as a natural instinct that is weakened by calculation. Inasmuch as men are not disinterested, they will look to their own interest before the interests of others; democracy encourages this by throwing each man on his own resources. One democratic man will come to another's aid if to do so involves no loss or injury to himself. For the spirit of compassion to become fully effective, society would require not only a condition of equality, but also a condition of plenty, or at least its equivalent in the minds of men. I have already mentioned the forces within democracy that work against such a possibility.

Furthermore, compassion, as a natural instinct, tends to undermine bonds that are merely conventional, and Tocqueville believes political society to be based on such bonds. The gentleness, softening of manners, and air of humanity that characterize democratic societies are not altogether unmixed blessings; they are apt to be more strongly felt within the family than between citizens. "Democracy," Tocqueville tells us, "loosens social ties, but tightens natural ones; it brings kindred more closely together, while it throws citizens more apart."[i] In effect, the spirit of compassion rein-

---

[i] Tocqueville, *Democracy*, II, 208; cf. 311: "As in periods of equality no man is compelled to lend his assistance to his fellow men, *and none has any right to expect much support* from them, everyone is at once independent and powerless. These two conditions ... inspire the citizen of a democratic country

forces domesticity, and thus reinforces the atomism of democratic society.

The propensities of democratic man I have described—toward materialism, mediocrity, compassion, domesticity, and isolation—these propensities, arising or gathering their strength from equality of conditions and individualism, constitute the core of Tocqueville's characterization of democracy. A regime under which their effects were not somehow mitigated would be one in which little opportunity would be available for the exercise of higher human faculties, one in which society would stagnate and public virtues languish altogether. Nor is this all. These same propensities make democratic man all too prone to accept or to drift into what Tocqueville labels a "soft" despotism. The fundamental paradox of democracy, as he understands it, is that equality of conditions is compatible with tyranny as well as with freedom. A species of equality can coexist with the greatest inequality. Left to its own devices, democracy is actually prone to the establishment of tyranny, whether of one over all, of the many over the few, or even of all over all.

The passion of democratic ages is for equality. It arises from the prevailing social condition, which, as we have seen, is the fundamental source of almost all the passions, ideas, and manners of society. But the drive for equality overpowers the desire for all else, even liberty. At first, Tocqueville throws up his hands in despair of discovering the roots or the source of strength of this drive. He resorts to a bald statement that it exists, that it is simply a fact of our times: "Do not ask what singular charm the men of democratic ages find in being equal, or what special reasons they may

---

with very contrary propensities. His independence fills him with self-reliance and pride among his equals; his debility makes him feel from time to time the want of some outward assistance, *which he cannot expect from any of them, because they are all impotent and unsympathizing* [*impuissants et froids*]." (Italics mine.)

have for clinging so tenaciously to equality rather than to
the other advantages that society holds out to them: equality
is the distinguishing characteristic of the age they live in;
that of itself is enough to explain that they prefer it to all
the rest."[47] Yet he proceeds at once to explain why most
men will invariably prefer equality to freedom. Liberty is
gained by vigilant effort; it is difficult to attain and easily
lost. Moreover, its excesses are apparent to all, while its benefits may easily escape detection. The advantages of equality,
on the other hand, are immediately felt. In one of his finest
passages, Tocqueville reveals the intimate connection between equality and pleasure:

> Political liberty bestows exalted pleasures from time to time
> upon a certain number of citizens. Equality every day confers a
> number of small enjoyments on every man. The charms of
> equality are every instant felt and are within the reach of all;
> the noblest hearts are not insensible to them, and the most vulgar
> souls exult in them. The passion that equality creates must there-
> fore be at once strong and general. Men cannot enjoy political
> liberty unpurchased by some sacrifices, and they never obtain it
> without great exertions. But the pleasures of equality are self-
> proffered; each of the petty incidents of life seems to occasion
> them, and in order to taste them, nothing is required but to live.[48]

If this is true, the shortcomings of equality may not be evident at all, except perhaps to those who have not been be-
numbed by its delights. At any rate, equality of conditions
has unleashed a passion that will not be put down; every
government of the future must acknowledge the source of
its energy in this omnipotent drive. The passion of men of
democratic communities for equality is "ardent, insatiable,
incessant, invincible; they call for equality in freedom; and
if they cannot obtain that, they still call for equality in
slavery."[49]

Love for equality may express itself in either of two

forms: a "manly and lawful passion" that seeks to raise all men to the level of the great, or a "depraved taste" that strives to reduce them to the lowest common denominator.[50] Obviously, if the former passion for equality were to prevail, the power of the objections to democracy would be appreciably reduced. But the forces at work under conditions of equality offer little hope that the manly passion for equality will triumph. The competition for material gain is so intense that each man has little likelihood of realizing his ambitions. Moreover, all men are not equally fitted for the race to satisfy their desires; all other things being equal, the victory inevitably goes to those of superior ability. All cannot be raised to the level of the great, for differences of ability come from God, or from nature. Democracy thus awakens a consciousness of the equal right of all to the advantages of this world, but frustrates men in attaining them. As long as freedom prevails, the struggle will go on unceasingly. Men of democratic times seek relief from this tension in a solution that at once gratifies their most intense desire and relieves them of the anguish to which it gives rise. Equality thus prepares man for the surrender of his freedom in the name of equality itself.

To Tocqueville, the form that this surrender might take ranges from capitulation to a despot of the time-honored description to the more subtle subservience to the tyranny of the majority. Viewed in this way, his famous account of the tyranny of the majority may be seen as a description of a particular form of the new despotism. Common to all its forms is a surrender of the self-governing capacity, a retreat from individualism, and an escape (or at least an attempt to escape) from the psychological duress engendered by equality of conditions. At first, Tocqueville appears to have thought that an old-style despot would be the most likely recipient of the power that the masses would either surren-

der or passively allow to slip from their hands, and of course
he never dismisses this possibility altogether. But as he considered it again, his thought took a new turn: terms like
"despotism" and "tyranny" became almost inadequate, and
he finally fell back on description to convey his meaning.[51]
In a society in which all are equal, independent, and impotent, power naturally gravitates to one center—the state—
that is especially anxious and able to accept and supervise
the surrender of freedom. There is no thought here of the
state in the grip of a power-hungry individual or clique. Instead, the state is a benevolent, faceless and impersonal ser-
vant of the people, more often than not taking the form of
a vast bureaucracy. Tocqueville calls attention to the increasing centralization of governments, to the growth of immense
tutelary powers standing ready to assume the burden of governing and providing for the comfort and well-being of their
citizens. Democratic men, he warns, will abandon their freedom to these mighty authorities in exchange for a "soft" despotism, one that "provides for their security, foresees and
supplies their necessities, facilitates their pleasures, manages
their principal concerns, directs their industry," and ultimately, spares them "all the care of thinking and all the
trouble of living."[j]

Tocqueville foresaw that such a government was not inconsistent with popular sovereignty. The people might very
well support it: "They console themselves for being in tute-
lage by the reflection that they have chosen their own guard-
ians. Every man allows himself to be put in leading-strings,
because he sees that it is not a person or a class of persons,

---

[j] Tocqueville, *Democracy*, II, 336. It need hardly be remarked that certain
twentieth-century regimes that have been characterized by their self-styled devotion to egalitarianism have also been characterized by anything but a "soft"
despotism. Tocqueville was guilty of grossly underestimating man's capacity for
violence, and of failing to see how it could persist under the veneer of democratic compassion.

but the people at large who hold the end of his chain."[52] Democracy originates a new form of despotism, society tyrannizing over itself. The only limitation imposed on the central authority is that its rules and its power be uniform, and applied to all without distinction. Thus the principle of equality is, ironically, preserved to the very end. This restriction actually facilitates the establishment of despotism, for government is relieved of the responsibility for making inquiry "into an infinity of details, which must be attended to if rules have to be adapted to different men."[53]

There is a description of democratic despotism in the *Old Régime* that appears to refute the view that tyranny of the majority is a form of the new despotism. Prior to the French Revolution, the Economists had formulated a social order in which all class distinctions were to be abolished:

The nation was to be composed of individuals almost exactly alike and unconditionally equal. In this undiscriminated mass was to reside, theoretically, the sovereign power; yet it was to be carefully deprived of any means of controlling or even supervising the activities of its own government. For above it was a single authority, its mandatary, which was entitled to do anything and everything in its name without consulting it. This authority could not be controlled by public opinion since public opinion had no means of making itself heard . . . .[54]

What the blueprint makers failed to appreciate was that under equality of conditions public opinion, majority opinion more precisely, had hit on a more subtle means of getting its wishes attended to than any traditional form of "consultation." So pervasive is the sway of public opinion in a democracy that it sets the tone of the whole society, to the extent that the governors can scarcely come to have desires different from those of the governed. The governors, however much they think themselves independent of the masses, are nonetheless their servants. As Tocqueville expresses it, the "universal moderation moderates the sovereign himself."[55] And what the majority of the governed want is soft despotism.

From the time when Mill saw fit to challenge Tocqueville by remarking that it was "not easy to see what sort of minority it can be over which the majority can have any interest in tyrannizing," Tocqueville's account of the tyranny of the majority has not escaped criticism.[56] A hundred years ago the central issue was whether property owners had anything to fear from the propertyless masses. More recently, concern with majority tyranny has dropped off because of the alleged discovery that majorities do not govern at all; that is, that the real dangers to democratic government lie in the tyranny exercised by minority or special-interest groups.[57] Tocqueville dealt with the issue of property explicitly. Moreover, despite his awareness of the pleadings of special-interest groups, he continued to regard majority tyranny as a particular threat to democracy. He realized that the composition of the majority in a democracy frequently fluctuates, but he also realized that this fluctuation takes place within the context of settled convictions that are themselves more or less unchanging.[58] In this sense one can speak of a permanent majority within a democracy. Tocqueville reminds us: "Two things are surprising in the United States: the mutability of the greater part of human actions, and the singular stability of certain principles. Men are in constant motion; the mind of man appears almost unmoved."[59] There is a somewhat surprising confirmation of Tocqueville's position in Robert Dahl's *Preface to Democratic Theory*, a work whose primary contribution is to demonstrate that majority rule is mostly a myth, and that majority tyranny is consequently a myth also. But Dahl concedes that:

If the majority rarely rules on matters of specific policy, nevertheless the specific policies selected by a process of "minorities rule" probably lie most of the time within the bounds of consensus set by the important values of the politically active members of the society. . . . Politicians subject to elections must operate within the limits set both by their own values, as indoctrinated members of the society, and by the expectations about what policies they can adopt and still be reelected. In a sense, what we ordinarily describe as democratic "politics" is merely the chaff. It is the surface manifestation, representing superficial conflicts. Prior to politics, beneath it, enveloping it, restricting it, conditioning it, is the underlying consensus on policy that usually exists in the society among a predominant portion of the politically active members.[60]

Tocqueville devotes a chapter of the *Democracy* (it is six sentences long) to showing how "it can be strictly said that the people govern in the United States," even if they are not politically active in any direct sense. "It is evident that the opinions, the prejudices, the interests, and even the passions of the people are hindered by no permanent obstacles from exercising a perpetual influence on the daily conduct of affairs. In the United States the majority governs in the name of the people, as is the case in all countries in which the people are supreme."[61]

Two democratic minorities were of particular concern to Tocqueville, especially since the apparent homogeneity of democratic society might cause one to overlook what in fact were two ineradicable sources of heterogeneity that could easily serve as the target of majority tyranny. These were the more or less permanent minorities of intellect and of wealth. The origins of the first lie beyond the reach of man; moreover, beyond the question of capacity, the difficulties of attaining knowledge are such that men under democratic conditions will rarely have either the time, the patience, or the inclination to pursue it. Tocqueville envisages no revolutionary breakthrough in the means of education, no "profusion of easy methods and cheap science" sufficient to overcome the want of time and talent. As long as the people remain the people, i.e., the many, they will be obliged to earn their bread, and hence will lack the leisure that is necessary for the cultivation of knowledge. "It is therefore quite as difficult to imagine a state in which all the citizens are very well informed as a state in which they are all wealthy; these two difficulties are correlative."[k] It is true, of course, that Tocqueville did not envisage the fully automated, affluent society with its promise of virtually unrelieved leisure for everyone. Yet the realization of that leisure will not necessarily guarantee its fruitful use, and it seems doubtful that the innate differences between men will ever be eliminated.

If the people acknowledge these innate differences, it is certain that they dispute the significance of them. For the qualitative superiority of the few they substitute a superiority based on quantity: "The moral authority of the majority is partly based upon the notion that there is more intelligence and wisdom in a number of men united than in a single individual, and that the number of the legislators is more important than their quality."[62] This is a venerable argument; what is novel under equality of conditions is that the minority comes at last to assent to this assault on the intellect. Perhaps assent is the wrong word, for it implies conscious agreement. The power of the majority in a democracy is sufficient to erode the capacity for dissent, the ability to conceive and above all to act on an idea different from that of the herd. To hold an opinion contrary to that of the majority on an important matter is not merely imprudent or unavailing, but is felt, Tocqueville maintains, to degrade

---

[k] Tocqueville, *Democracy*, I, 207–8; cf. II, 43: "Nothing is more necessary to the culture of the higher sciences or of the more elevated departments of science than meditation; and nothing is less suited to meditation than the structure of democratic society. . . . In the midst of this universal tumult, this incessant conflict of jarring interests, this continual striving of men after fortune, where is that calm to be found which is necessary for the deeper combinations of the intellect?"

one as a human being: "The power of the majority is so absolute and irresistible that one must give up one's rights as a citizen and almost abjure one's qualities as a man if one intends to stray from the track which it prescribes."[63] This tyranny of the majority over the minds of its intellectual superiors accentuates the disposition of democracy toward conformity and mediocrity.

There remains the problem of the attitude of the majority toward those who possess property, a problem that cannot be reduced to a crude conflict between the haves and the have-nots. Tocqueville certainly tries to overcome the fears of those critics of democracy who saw in the rule of the many the inevitable destruction of all property rights; in the Preface to the *Democracy* he takes care to point out that in the most advanced democratic country in the world property rights have enjoyed greater guarantees than anywhere else. Still, he is not sanguine that the eternal struggle between the rich and the poor has been overcome by the democratic revolution—all have not been reduced or elevated to the same level of wealth, and the envy of the poor toward those in better circumstances has not been assuaged by whatever leveling has occurred. How secure, then, are the rights of property?

According to Tocqueville, the division between the few and the many, the rich and the poor, is a permanent feature of all societies, destined to remain despite the progressive realization of equality of conditions. This is a "fixed rule" to which all communities are subject.[64] On the other hand, the proportion of individuals within a society making up each of the three great orders—the wealthy, those of moderate means, and the poor—may vary from one society to another. Though the proportion may change, Tocqueville rejects the idea that the wealthy or the moderately wealthy may ever constitute a majority. "Universal suffrage, there-

fore, in point of fact does invest the poor with the government of society."[1] Once in a position of power, the poor will
rule in their own interest, as they understand it. But, as if
in anticipation of Mill's argument that common sense will
persuade the poor that their interest lies in respecting property, Tocqueville declares:

> In vain will it be objected that the true interest of the people
> is to spare the fortunes of the rich, since [the people] must suffer
> in the long run from the general impoverishment which will
> ensue. . . . If remote advantages had power to prevail over the
> passions and the exigencies of the moment, no such thing as a
> tyrannical sovereign or an exclusive aristocracy could ever exist.[65]

He sees, then, no reason to believe that the traditional conflict between rich and poor will cease under democratic conditions, or that the one will lack the will or the opportunity
to oppress the other. Since the majority are poor, and since
it is they who will be sovereign, the fears of the critics of
democracy are justified after all.

Yet how are we to reconcile this with apparently contradictory statements elsewhere in the *Democracy*? In the second part, for example, Tocqueville declares that in democratic communities the poor, instead of being a great majority, will be comparatively few in number, and that the new
middle classes will be in the majority. But the middle classes
own property and are, in fact, the foremost defenders of
property rights.[66] What, then, have the rich to fear from a
majority whose passions and interests are so similar to their
own?

It must be recalled that one of the fundamental discoveries of the modern era was that freeing the acquisitive instinct of man from the shackles of an unrealistic morality

---

[1] Tocqueville, *Democracy*, I, 222. Tocqueville uses the term "poor" in a rela-
tive, not in an absolute, sense; see 222*n*.

would make possible not only a proliferation of material goods, but also the enjoyment of an unprecedented degree of freedom from religious and secular authorities. It took a special breed of men to succeed in freeing that instinct, and the members of the new middle class that Tocqueville describes are not at all identical with those men, the "rational and industrious" men that Locke had in mind. They are rather more cautious, more timorous, more concerned with preserving what they have. They cannot shake the anxiety that to Tocqueville seems the earmark of democratic man, the anxiety that derives from the peculiar conditions of their pursuit of the good life:

> It may readily be conceived that if men passionately bent upon physical gratifications desire eagerly, they are also easily discouraged; as their ultimate object is to enjoy, the means to reach that object must be prompt and easy, or the trouble of acquiring the gratification will be greater than the gratification itself. Their prevailing frame of mind, then, is at once ardent and relaxed, violent and enervated. Death is often less dreaded by them than perseverance in continuous efforts to one end.[67]

Here, perhaps, is another link between the tyranny of the majority and the new despotism. The men who surrender to soft, comfortable despotism are the men of the new majority who have enjoyed the first rewards of the universal pursuit of well-being. But their desires have outrun their opportunities. Frightened at the prospect of losing what they have to those more able than themselves, the majority turn to government as the only power capable of protecting their rights and goods and of restraining the ambitions of the few.[m] At the expense of the few, the wealthy, the government secures

[m] By the same token, the new middle class is equally apprehensive of the socialistic inclinations, real or imagined, of the poor. As Salomon notes: "A new despotism arose because the bourgeois classes were willing to bow to any ruler, however legally questionable, who would protect their interests against the masses." ("Tocqueville, 1959," p. 470.)

to the many a modest enjoyment of the good things of this life, a policy that is not incompatible with protection of property rights on a limited scale.

The advent of a new type of despotism revives the ancient discussion of the good man and the good citizen. Aristotle had pointed out that except under the most fortuitous circumstances the two were not identical. The main point of his argument is that it is far easier to be a good citizen, since this requires only subservience to the principles of the regime under which one lives. Their goodness or badness is irrelevant: one could be a good citizen of a bad regime. To be a good man, however, one must live in a society that encourages the realization of man's moral and intellectual potentialities. It is barely conceivable that a good man might develop under a tyranny, but if he did it would be an instance of nature asserting herself over the normally sovereign way of life of the regime.

What Tocqueville discovered is that in a democracy, under certain conditions, it is easier to be a good man than a good citizen:

> True, democratic societies which are not free may well be prosperous, cultured, pleasing to the eye, and even magnificent, such is the sense of power implicit in their massive uniformity; in them may flourish many private virtues [*qualités*], good fathers, honest merchants, exemplary landowners, and good Christians, too. . . . But, I make bold to say, never shall we find under such conditions a great citizen, still less a great nation. . . ."[n]

Moreover, the decline of citizenship is not to be associated only with the appearance of the new despotism. Equality of

---

[n] Tocqueville, *Old Régime*, p. xiv; cf. *Democracy*, II, 347: "It would seem as if the rulers of our time sought only to use men in order to make things great; I wish that they would try a little more to make great men; that they would set less value on the work and more upon the workman; that they would never forget that a nation cannot long remain strong when every man belonging to it is individually weak; and that no form or combination of social polity has yet been devised to make an energetic people out of a community of pusillanimous and enfeebled citizens."

conditions, as we have seen, even if accompanied by some freedom naturally generates a disposition to forsake the public arena for private life.[68] This development, which Tocqueville associates with democracy, may have arisen from ideas that were the common stock of the political philosophers of the modern era. From Machiavelli to Locke there is an unprecedented celebration of what we have come to regard as the private sector. Some philosophers encouraged and protected this sphere (which necessarily included within it a certain degree of freedom) as a means of increasing or strengthening the security of the sovereign; others adopted the same scheme for directly opposite reasons, seeing in the security of the individual's private pursuits the only protection against unwarranted encroachments by the sovereign. Whatever the motivation of its midwives, the liberal era had been born, with its division of political life into public and private spheres and its frank acknowledgment of the superiority of the latter. At the heart of the liberal tradition, ultimately, is the doctrine of natural rights. Its initial acceptance led to what Leo Strauss has called "the first crisis of modernity," when some philosophers, most notably Rousseau, warned that this doctrine would cause the demise of all those virtues and qualities associated with patriotism and public-spiritedness. The neglect of any concern with the whole, of any genuine identification with the fatherland, turned men into "bourgeois rather than citizens."[69] It mattered little that these bourgeois manifested the ordinary traits of decency: moderation in their appetites, faithfulness to their obligations, respect for civil peace and order. It mattered little, in other words, that they were good men. What was essential was that they be transformed into citizens.[o]

As I have mentioned earlier, Tocqueville consistently

[o] In the *Old Régime,* Tocqueville had stressed the connection between material well-being and individualism: "Eighteenth-century man had little of that

elevates political considerations above all others. It is not surprising, then, that he should prefer the good citizen to the good man, even to the extent of finding the great citizen more praiseworthy (his path being strewn with greater obstacles) than the good Christian. The superiority of public life over private pursuits is everywhere assumed in Tocqueville's work: it is evident in his praise of such grandiose exploits as the civilizing missions of the English in India or of the French in Algeria, in his frank acknowledgment of the uses of war, and in his undisguised admiration for the dedication of aristocratic regimes to political purposes. In the *Democracy* he had posed this apparently rhetorical choice:

> We must first understand what is wanted of society and its government. . . . Would you constitute a people fitted to act powerfully upon all other nations, and prepared for those high enterprises which, whatever be their results, will leave a name forever famous in history? If you believe such to be the principal object of society, avoid the government of the democracy, for it would not lead you with certainty to the goal. . . . If, in short, you are of the opinion that the principal object of a government is not to confer the greatest possible power and glory upon the body of the nation, but to ensure the greatest enjoyment and to avoid the most misery to each of the individuals who compose it— if such be your desire, then equalize the conditions of men and establish democratic institutions.[70]

Yet Tocqueville never resigned himself to either of these alternatives: he did not believe that democracy was simply

---

craving for material well-being which leads the way to servitude. A craving which, while morally debilitating, can be singularly tenacious and insidious, it often operates in close association with such private virtues as family love, a sense of decorum, respect for religion, and even a lukewarm but punctilious observance of the rites of the established Church. While promoting moral rectitude, it rules out heroism and excels in making people well-behaved but mean-spirited as citizens" (p. 118).

inevitable, nor did he believe that under democratic conditions one had to relinquish all hope of greatness. He had no illusions on this score; he understood better than any man before him how the forces released by equality vitiated men's devotion to causes that bore only indirectly on their own well-being. For example, should a "bold innovator" arise to rouse the people from their apathy, Tocqueville predicts this reception:

To his vehemence they secretly oppose their inertia, to his revolutionary tendencies their conservative interests, their homely tastes to his adventurous passions, their good sense to the flights of his genius, to his poetry their prose. With immense exertion he raises them for an instant, but they speedily escape from him and fall back, as it were, by their own weight. He strains himself to rouse the indifferent and distracted multitude and finds at last that he is reduced to impotence, not because he is conquered, but because he is alone.[71]

The quotation is taken from Tocqueville's chapter on revolutions in democratic times, and "innovator" might be construed as meaning a mere adventurer, perhaps even a self-seeking demagogue. Tocqueville has, of course, no sympathy for such men, but neither has he any for a society in which there is constant experimentation with secondary matters, such as the material conditions of life, but in which people carefully refrain from touching whatever is fundamental in religion, morals, or politics. If citizens shy away from this kind of soul-searching, if every fundamental innovation is considered incitement to revolution, any genuine growth may be jeopardized:

If men continue to shut themselves more closely within the narrow circle of domestic interests, and to live on that kind of excitement, it is to be apprehended that they may ultimately become inaccessible to those great and powerful public emotions which perturb nations, but which develop them and recruit them.

When property becomes so fluctuating and the love of property so restless and so ardent, I cannot but fear that men may arrive at such a state as to regard every new theory as a peril, every innovation as an irksome toil, [and] every social improvement as a stepping-stone to revolution, and so refuse to move altogether for fear of being moved too far. I dread, and I confess it, lest they should at last so entirely give way to a cowardly love of present enjoyment as to lose sight of the interests of their future selves and those of their descendants, and prefer to glide along the easy current of life rather than to make, when it is necessary, a strong and sudden effort to a higher purpose.[72]

If Tocqueville continues to maintain that equality of conditions will not lead men and nations "with certainty" to a human life compatible with greatness, he must also mean that this goal, though difficult, is not unreachable. We are led once again to the dichotomy between democracy and human excellence, the permanence and intransigence of which he refused to acknowledge. Every regime in the past that showed signs of excellence or greatness was tarnished at its core by its hostility to the requirements of natural justice. A genuine integration of justice and excellence would approximate a total solution of the human problem. To discover how future regimes may realize this objective is, I believe, Tocqueville's enterprise. Resolving the problem of democracy requires finding a place within democracy for liberty, for human excellence, for a renaissance of public virtue, and for the possibility of greatness. It has been said that Plato's objective in the *Republic* was to construct a society that would be safe for philosophy; in a similar vein, Harold Laski has written of Tocqueville, "There is a fascinating sense in which the whole effort of his thought was to discover the secret of a social order in which there was scope for the manner of man he himself was."[73]

III

The Problem of Democracy Resolved

A GENERATION after the appearance of the *Democracy* Lincoln was to apply to the solution of American problems an understanding of democracy paralleling that of Tocqueville. Both rejected the view identified with men like Adams and Hamilton: that democracy stood in need of correction through essentially aristocratic measures; for example, the addition of a legislative branch drawing its members from an aristocratic class. As Professor Jaffa describes it, "Lincoln grasped the necessity of evolving aristocratic restraints upon democracy not by borrowing contra-democratic devices from a non-democratic past, but by evolving them from within the democratic ethos as perfections of that ethos."[1] It was to forestall the Hamiltons of his own day that Tocqueville wrote in the conclusion of the *Democracy*:

I find that a great number of my contemporaries undertake to make a selection from among the institutions, the opinions, and the ideas that originated in the aristocratic constitution of society as it was; a portion of these elements they would willingly relinquish, but they would keep the remainder and transplant them into their new world. I fear that such men are wasting their time and their strength in virtuous but unprofitable efforts. The object is not to retain the peculiar advantages which the inequality of conditions bestows upon mankind, but to secure the new benefits which equality may supply. We have not to seek to make ourselves like our progenitors, but to strive to work out that species of greatness and happiness which is our own.[2]

The problem of democracy must be resolved, then, on the level of democracy; that is to say, its resolution must be perfectly consonant with equality, the principle of democracy. While this principle prevails, not even a despot could rule without making his obeisance to it. Those who have no despotic aspirations, but rather seek to preserve freedom for themselves and their fellow citizens, must of course do the same.

No legislator is wise or powerful enough to preserve free institutions if he does not take equality for his first principle and his watchword. All of our contemporaries who would establish or secure the independence and the dignity of their fellow men must show themselves the friends of equality, and the only worthy means of showing themselves as such is to be so; upon this depends the success of their holy enterprise.[3]

Clearly, Tocqueville is not guilty of vulgar acquiescence to the principles of the prevailing regime. He seeks nothing less than a great social and political order erected on the only just foundation.

It would not be altogether facetious to suggest that Tocqueville understood the problem of democracy, and its solution, in terms of a simple formula: equality was the cause; freedom, the remedy. "To combat the evils which equality may produce, there is only one effectual remedy: namely, political freedom."[4] This approach is compatible with a realization of the subtleties and complexities of political life, and with an awareness that politics results from many diverse causes rather than any single one. Like other nineteenth-century theorists, Tocqueville was in revolt against those of his predecessors who had looked on political things in an abstract way. To them, the political realm was like a geometrical system more or less deducible from a few simple axioms of human behavior. Hobbes and Locke had thought of civil society as developing, in accordance with these axioms, from a simple state of nature in which men possessed certain natural rights. However,

Tocqueville (like Rousseau and Burke) placed equal stress on the influences of custom, tradition, historical continuity, religion, climate, and topography—in fine, on the situation of man in particular circumstances. Thus he could recommend various social and political institutions to meet the needs of particular situations: for example, the federal system, while perhaps appropriate in America, would be calamitous in France.

Tocqueville never said that equality was the cause of everything in democratic times; he said it was the primary fact. Considerations of custom, religion, and the like were important to the extent that they helped implement and strengthen the passion for freedom. Liberty—political liberty—is the ingredient that, if added to the democratic compound of equality and materialism, can prevent the degeneration into mediocrity and domesticity, and even into despotism, that Tocqueville feared. If it is the atomism of democratic society that breeds the sense of impotence and apathy that in turn sets the stage for tyranny, what democratic society needs is a cohesive force that can reawaken a sense of political responsibility and interdependence. Such a force is freedom.

Only freedom can deliver the members of a community from that isolation which is the lot of the individual left to his own devices . . . [and, by] compelling them to get in touch with each other, [can] promote an active sense of fellowship. In a community of free citizens every man is daily reminded of the need of meeting his fellow men, of hearing what they have to say, of exchanging ideas and coming to an agreement as to the conduct of their common interests.[5]

The irony of the democratic predicament is that democracy encourages men to surrender their liberty, the one thing essential to their deliverance. However, when Tocqueville surveys the forces at work under democratic conditions, he finds reason not to be altogether pessimistic. Although a condition of equality may be said to contain the germs of its own degeneracy, it also contains the seeds of its own redemption:

> The principle of equality, which makes men independent of each other, gives them a habit and a taste for following in their private actions no other guide than their own will. This complete independence, which they constantly enjoy in regard to their equals and in the intercourse of private life, tends to make them look upon all authority with a jealous eye and speedily suggests to them the notion and the love of political freedom. Men living at such times have a natural bias toward free institutions. . . . Far from finding fault with equality because it inspires a spirit of independence, I praise it primarily for that very reason. I admire it because it lodges in the very depths of each man's mind and heart that indefinable feeling, the instinctive inclination for political independence, and thus prepares the remedy for the ill which it engenders.[6]

The passion for equality at any cost is confronted, then, by a passion for freedom. Nevertheless, the first is stronger; moreover, the passion that induces a man to turn concern for his own welfare over to a government is augmented in its effect by omnipresent tendencies toward centralization of government. Tocqueville sees governments as becoming every day more powerful, and individuals more helpless. If men do nothing at all, centralization and an accompanying erosion of local initiative will be the natural outcome.[7]

To counteract this tendency and to strengthen the struggling forces of freedom, Tocqueville employs the tools and techniques of politics: enlightenment, persuasion, invention, and myth. Only if the art of politics can be brought to the aid of freedom can the problem of democracy be resolved. This, Tocqueville found, had been accomplished with consummate skill in America. The Americans had applied to democracy remedies of their own invention, and although these remedies had not given rise to "the only imaginable democratic laws or the most perfect which it is possible to conceive,"[8] they had provided "useful data" for those who wished to resolve the problem. American experience suggests for the resolution of the democratic problem "democratic expedients" such as local self-government, separation of church and state, a free press, indirect elections, an independent judiciary, and the encouragement of various associations for the pursuit of various social and political ends. Tocqueville does not simply recommend the adoption of each and every American practice—to take the federal system again, he believed it to be much too complicated to suit the temperament and realities of European political life. "A proposition must be plain," he reminds us, "to be adopted by the understanding of a people. A false notion which is clear and precise will always have more power in the world than a true principle which is obscure or involved."[9]

Opinion about the effectiveness of the various democratic expedients or devices may change from time to time, but we are familiar with them all; there is no need to dwell on them. What is not clear is the purpose they are meant to serve, and the principle from which they derive their power to accomplish it. Their purpose, I suggest, is nothing less than the transformation of the atoms of democratic society into citizens, into men whose first thought is not of their private interest, but of the common good. To the degree that these devices succeed, individuals will cease to think only of themselves; their characters will have been transformed. Kant could write in *Perpetual Peace* of organizing a state in which the interaction of men's private interests "either annihilates or moderates their injurious effect, and, by rendering it null to reason, forces man to be, if not a good moral being, at least a good citizen."[10] Tocqueville, however, thought it impossible to devise a regime whose institutions would produce good laws by the interaction of men who were wholly thoughtless, or driven by improper motives. Late in life, Tocqueville again expressed his sentiments on institutions (perhaps "mechanisms" or "devices" would better convey his meaning), and these sentiments do not depart at all from his intention in the *Democracy*:

I consider institutions as exercising only a secondary influence over the destinies of man. Would to God that I could believe them to be all powerful. I would have more hopes for our future, for we might someday chance to stumble upon the precious recipe which would cure all our ills, or upon a man acquainted with the nostrum. But alas! there is no such thing; and I am convinced that the excellence of political societies does not depend upon their laws, but upon what they are prepared to become by their sentiments, principles, and opinions, the moral and intellectual qualities given by nature and education to the men of whom [societies] consist.[11]

He does not consider, then, any simple affirmation of the principle of *Federalist 51*, for example, which secures the prerogatives of the separate branches of government by the device of playing the respective officeholders off against one another. The democratic devices Tocqueville has in mind must make men moral, that is, must make them citizens. In the extreme, these devices would make men selfless. Ironically, they pursue this end by relying on self-interest, albeit self-interest rightly understood. But of this, later.

Tocqueville resorts to democratic devices, then, in an attempt to force a sense of public morality to evolve out of the spirit of extreme individualism characterizing democratic ages. He begins with the familiar call for administrative decentralization, to foster individual activity on matters important to the local community or township. The adoption of the jury system touches each man with direct responsibility for the liberty of his fellows. Large groups of men united for a common purpose will, he believes, inevitably emerge: professional associations, such as the bar or medicine; associations formed for the transmission of news and ideas; mass political parties. Associations of all descriptions will proliferate. At the lowest level, each man will be most directly involved, but the scope of his activity will be most sharply restricted. The larger associations may act on a grand scale, but the involvement of each of their members will be minimal. In this respect, despite Tocqueville's frequent affirmation of associations as democratic substitutes for aristocracy, they are only quasi-aristocratic. An association may fulfill some of the functions of an aristocracy, but it can scarcely provide each of its members with the same sense of individual responsibility that was possible for at least the leaders of the aristocracy. A member of a vast association may not perceive, under certain circumstances, any diminution of his sense of isolation. This suggests that mere membership in a group does not change men: it must be the process of acting jointly with others that works to remake character.

Extreme as it may seem, and with whatever reservations may have to be introduced later, Tocqueville's objective has never been as well stated as in this passage from the *Social Contract*:

He who dares to undertake the making of a people's institutions ought to feel himself capable, so to speak, of changing human nature: of transforming each individual, who is by himself a complete and solitary whole, into part of a greater whole from which he in a manner receives his life and being; of altering man's constitution for the purpose of strengthening it; and of substituting a partial and moral existence for the physical and independent existence nature has conferred on us all. He must, in a word, take away from man his own resources and give him instead new ones alien to him, and incapable of being made use of without the help of other men. The more completely these natural resources are annihilated, the greater and the more lasting are those which he acquires, and the more stable and perfect the new institutions; so that if each citizen is nothing and can do nothing without the rest, and the resources acquired by the whole are equal or superior to the aggregate of the resources of all the individuals, it may be said that legislation is at the highest possible point of perfection.[12]

Although Tocqueville hardly suggests "annihilating" man's original nature, he frequently praises the men of the past who worked to change it.[18] But such changes can arise only through a frank recognition of man's natural proclivities. This is the meaning of his reliance on self-interest rightly understood. His ultimate objective, however, remains the same as Rousseau's.

Let us consider the democratic devices of local self-government and local initiative. To counteract the effects of centralization, and to train each citizen in the theory and practice of freedom, Tocqueville proposes an increase in autonomy at the township and community level. By learning to care about and cooperate on political matters that affect him directly, each citizen is to acquire the rudiments of public responsibility. The township is thus the locus of the transformation of self-interest into patriotism, at least into a species of patriotism. That Tocqueville relies mainly on enlightened self-interest may be seen from this account:

It is difficult to draw a man out of his own circle to interest him in the destiny of the state, because he does not clearly understand what influence the destiny of the state can have upon his own lot. But if it is proposed to make a road cross the end of his estate, he will see at a glance that there is a connection between this small public affair and his greatest private affairs; and he will discover, without its being shown to him, the close tie that unites private to general interest. Thus, by entrusting to the citizens the administration of minor affairs, [rather] than by surrendering to them in the control of important ones, far more may be done toward interesting them in the public welfare and convincing them that they constantly stand in need of one another in order to provide for it.[14]

The kind of patriotism generated by the exercise of freedom on the local level is an outgrowth of individual self-concern, one of the passions democracy emancipates. "The feeling [democratic man] entertains toward the state is analogous to that which unites him to his family, and it is by a kind of selfishness that he interests himself in the welfare of his country."[15] But this feeling, which has its origins in a selfish impulse, is ultimately converted into a selfless attitude or state of character. "Men attend to the interests of the public first by necessity, afterward by choice; what was intentional becomes an instinct, and by dint of working for the good of one's fellow citizens, the habit and the taste for serving them are at length acquired." Even aspirants for public office learn to consider the wishes of their fellow citizens from "ambitious motives," and thus discover that it is in their own interest "to forget themselves."[16]

The same process can be seen at work in many of the other devices Tocqueville recommended. The jury system typically turns the attention of men to the affairs of others, and, by so doing, "rubs off that private selfishness which is the rust of society."[17] Political associations teach men "to surrender their own will to that of all the rest and to make their own exertions subordinate to the common impulse"; in this process, such associations function as "large free schools, where all the members of the community go to learn the general theory of association."[18]

The generation of a sense of public concern does not exhaust the possibilities of these devices. They may also teach men to make public decisions wisely and well. The jury system may improve the quality of decision-making; and a device such as separation of powers may moderate or restrain the passions of the many for a time, so that wiser counsel may prevail. The roles of some free institutions may be passive, but by no means unimportant:

The great utility of popular institutions is to sustain liberty during those intervals wherein the human mind is otherwise occupied—to give it a kind of vegetative life, which may keep it in existence during those periods of inattention. The forms of a free government allow men to become temporarily weary of their liberty without losing it. When a people are determined to be slaves, it is impossible to hinder their becoming so; but by free institutions they may be sustained for some time in independence, even without their own assistance.[19]

The jury system is an example of the general and pervasive role Tocqueville expected members of the legal profession to play in a democracy. The training that lawyers in particular receive gives them a taste for order, for legal and political forms, and for the connection of ideas—a taste that distinguishes them from the multitude and gives an aristocratic turn to their thinking and preferences. They tend to be conservative and antidemocratic, and to the extent that they play a prominent role in society (as they are bound to in a society where almost every political question is eventually transformed into a legal issue) they temper the tastes and passions of the many. However, Tocqueville was not oblivious to the shortcomings of the legal profession. Legal training, backed up by whatever good intentions, does not lead to the disinterested pursuit of wisdom or even of justice, for the law may sometimes be blind to the highest considerations. Thus he remarks that lawyers prefer legality and public order to freedom, are "superstitiously" attached to tradition, and are generally narrow and inflexible in their opinions. An implicit fear is recurrent in his thought, the fear that respect for legal forms per se is not incompatible with despotism. Nevertheless, he thought it essential to preserve in or adapt to the democratic condition whatever elements might instill a respect for form and orderly procedure in the majority, and thus restrain its passions.[a]

Of all the democratic devices, freedom of association is most important.[b] As in former ages the aristocracy protected the liberties of the people against the encroachments of the sovereign, so in a democracy associations protect the rights of minorities against the tyranny of the majority.[20] Since each man in a democracy is independent but also impotent, he may only oppose the views of the majority by associating with others. This is one political function of the natural right of association. But the utility of associations goes far beyond mere political considerations. Participation in political groups reveals the advantages of associations for other purposes—educational, scientific, commercial—and engenders a taste for them. Tocqueville gives associations a dignity that is perhaps novel in political thought. Whereas most earlier theorists had thought that parties, factions, or

[a] It should be noted that the role Tocqueville assigns to lawyers in resolving the problem of democracy is an apparent breach of the principle that the resolution must be made on the level of democracy; but it is, after all, only a partial breach. Despite lawyers' aristocratic tastes and habits, they are bound to the people by birth and interest, and thus do not constitute a distinct class. At best, lawyers are *quasi*-aristocrats. See *Democracy*, I, 285f, 289.

[b] I shall not stop to consider freedom of the press, which Tocqueville sees as an association for the circulation of ideas and opinions. His attitude toward freedom of the press is not altogether consistent. At one point he opposes censorship not on theoretical grounds, but because a system free from abuse cannot be devised. At another he introduces a theoretical argument against censorship: that a free press is an inevitable consequence of the idea of the sovereignty of the people. See *ibid.*, pp. 188–90.

associations were divisive of society, Tocqueville thought that they were absolutely essential for democratic society's well-being. He maintained that associations, far from contributing to the destruction of social unity, overcome the divisive propensities of democracy: that by organizing and operating associations, men learn the art of adapting themselves to a common purpose. According to Tocqueville, learning to associate is the prerequisite for the preservation of civilization itself: "A people among whom individuals lost the power of achieving great things single-handed, without acquiring the means of producing them by united exertions, would soon relapse into barbarism."[21] Tocqueville thus sees in associations a means not only of mitigating the tyranny of the majority, but also of overcoming the mediocrity to which democracy is prone.

Still, the right of association is not without its drawbacks, mainly because of its disturbing propensity for keeping the political world in a state of agitation. Tocqueville warns repeatedly: "It cannot be denied that the unrestrained liberty of association for political purposes is the last degree of liberty which a people is fit for. If it does not throw them into anarchy, it perpetually brings them, as it were, to the verge of it."[22] Curiously, although America has carried the right of association further than any other nation it has not been plagued by the instability one might expect. In explanation Tocqueville offers the following, reminiscent in its own way of the argument of *Federalist 10*:

If . . . you survey the infinite number of trading companies in operation in the United States, and perceive that the Americans are on every side unceasingly engaged in the execution of important and difficult plans, which the slightest revolution would throw into confusion, you will readily comprehend why people so well employed are by no means tempted to perturb the state or to destroy that public tranquillity by which they all profit.[23]

Without stability there is no prospect of preserving the fruits of these other, chiefly commercial, enterprises. On balance, Tocqueville believes that political associations must come first, both in importance and in time. Americans "*afterwards* transfer to civil life the notions they have thus acquired, and make them subservient to a thousand purposes. Thus it is by the enjoyment of a dangerous freedom that the Americans learn the art of rendering the dangers of freedom less formidable."[24]

It is important, I think, to keep in mind that the function of all Tocqueville's democratic expedients is the making of citizens, a complex process that involves the growth in each man not only of a consciousness of others, but also of a perception of the common good and the ways by which it may be fostered. I do not believe Tocqueville's promotion of associations was equivalent to a defense of simple pluralism. Thus, I believe Seymour Lipset's emphasis is misleading when he remarks: "[Tocqueville's] study of America suggested to him two institutions which might combat the new leviathan: local self-government and voluntary associations. Involvement in such institutions seemed to him a condition for the stability of the democratic system. By disseminating ideas and creating consensus among their members, they become the basis for conflict between one organization and another."[25] It is true that the institutions I have described are designed to promote stability, among other things, but I do not believe Tocqueville thought of them primarily as "the mechanisms for creating and maintaining the consensus necessary for a democratic society."[26] He was aware of the danger to the common good arising from the development of unequal "particular" wills within the state, as his fear of the growth of manufacturing interests reveals. He would also have agreed with Rousseau that the more associations there are, the less likely it is that one will be able to dominate the others.[o] Nevertheless, Tocqueville does not suggest that the common good will emerge from a contest between the many wills represented by the principal associations of the nation. Encouraging the growth of civil and commercial associations may, of course, produce peace and public order by occupying the citizenry with interests not likely to disturb the nation. But Tocqueville sought more than peace and public order—at the very least, a sense of patriotism or devotion to the common good; above and beyond this, an urge to greatness. His democratic expedients are designed to make the realization of these goals possible. That they are worthy goals is assumed, as is the existence of the prerequisites for achieving them—the existence especially of a fundamental consensus about what constitutes the common good.

The existence of this prior assumption becomes obvious after a close look at Tocqueville's appeal to local institutions. Their effectiveness in generating a sense of patriotism depends on each citizen's ability to comprehend the common good, his own interest, and the connection between them. The process by which patriotism is generated at the local level is valuable to Tocqueville because it brings about a harmony of the common good and private interest, or overcomes whatever disharmony may have been thought to exist. But the process itself cannot account for the origin of the concept of the common good; in fact, the process is comprehensible only on the prior assumption that a common good exists, that it is intelligible, and that it is superior to private interest. This assumption underlies the whole of Tocqueville's political thought.

Faguet makes an especially serious criticism of Tocqueville's reliance on local institutions. Contrasting town gov-

---

[o] Cf. Rousseau, p. 23: "If there are partial societies, it is best to have as many as possible, and to prevent them from being unequal. . . ."

ernment under an aristocracy and under a democracy, he
says: "A town administered by its notables could, in the
long run, be governed not only wisely but *politically*—that
is to say, in the general interests of the nation."[27] Were a
town administered by its citizens, would they be able to rise
above their provincialism to a concern with the national interest? How would they distinguish national from local interest? Tocqueville not only does not provide a simple formula to distinguish matters concerning the general interest,
and thus properly belonging to the national government,
from matters that may safely be left to local authorities:[d]
he recognizes that if a nation is subject to significant external pressures, local autonomy in anything other than trivial
matters is impossible. In such a case, the distinction between
national and local becomes arbitrary and meaningless. As
Faguet (writing in the nineteenth century) sees it, local autonomy presents no danger

in a country like America, which does not have to make external
war and which has, consequently, no *need for an intense national
life*; but it is immensely dangerous in a country whose perpetual
objective, whether it likes it or not, is and must be possible war-
fare; and all the European countries are in this pass. The bor-
oughs' money, the provinces' money, this supplies the war-chest,
which must not be drained, wasted or imperiled by them. But
why should they be supposed to be prodigal? They are not; they
spend in accordance with their resources; but they think only,
and can think only, of their own resources and needs. The State
alone is the State, and can think of general needs, future perils,
international complications; and, in consideration of these things,
can oblige provinces to be economical not in accordance with
their need, but with its own.

In this way, the most local administration is already politics,

---

[d] See *Democracy*, I, 89ff, 398ff. Some matters, such as the regulation of civil
and political rights, are of "mixed" character, and in principle may be regulated
either by the national or the local authorities as circumstances permit or require.

and politics of a most important and miscellaneous character in the general interest. . . .*

Tocqueville foresaw another obstacle to the effective functioning of local institutions: that as society becomes more complex it becomes less able to accommodate local autonomy. "A highly civilized community can hardly tolerate a local independence, is disgusted at its numerous blunders, and is apt to despair of success before the experiment is completed."[28] Reflecting on the absence of any genuine local freedom in Europe he adds, with almost a note of despair: "Municipal freedom is not the fruit of human efforts; it is rarely created by others, but is, as it were, secretly self-produced in the midst of a semi-barbarous state of society."[29] This is an exaggeration, of course, as is made clear by his affirmation toward the end of the *Democracy* that "in the democratic ages which are opening upon us, individual independence and local liberties will ever be the products of art."[30] But he has no illusions, for the attempt to establish local liberties will be opposed everywhere by the natural tendencies of democracy: "Not only is a democratic people led by its own taste to centralize its government, but the passions of all the men by whom it is governed constantly urge it in the same direction."[31] Another critic, Maxime Leroy, investigates the consequences of this dilemma:

The fate of these local liberties so ardently defended is dependent upon an effort which must go constantly against the natural movement of democratic societies. Will a democratic society be able . . . to struggle continuously against its own nature? . . . In trusting to political art for the success of such an enterprise are we not, from Tocqueville's own point of view, endeavoring to destroy this same nature of things and to substitute for it a purely artificial work?[32]

---

* Faguet, p. 100. For a statement of the same problem applied to contemporary America, see Jaffa, "The Case for a Stronger National Government," pp. 106–25.

The question is apt, but Leroy fails to see that Tocqueville's "artificial" devices are entirely compatible with certain indelible features of democratic conditions—the passion for self-interest in particular. True to his insistence that the problem of democracy must be solved on the level of democracy, Tocqueville is bent on evolving democratic restraints that have their foundation in democracy. The application of the doctrine of self-interest rightly understood is the archetype of all such procedures.

In the introduction to the *Democracy*, Tocqueville tells us that the poor have "adopted the doctrine of self-interest as the rule of [their] actions without understanding the science that puts it to use; and [their] selfishness is no less blind than was formerly [their] devotion to others."[33] Blind selfishness must now be replaced by enlightened selfishness, and to this end Tocqueville proceeds to develop a "science" of enlightened self-interest. The elaboration of the doctrine of self-interest rightly understood is offered in a very brief chapter of the *Democracy*, one whose importance cannot be measured by its length. Whereas he typically preserves an air of studied impartiality, in this chapter he explicitly offers his own judgment of the doctrine. Moreover, he does so after remarking that he might very well have used the difficulty of the subject as an excuse for not committing himself.

I am not afraid to say that the doctrine of self-interest rightly understood appears to me the best suited of all philosophical theories to the wants of the men of our time, and that I regard it as their chief remaining security against themselves. Towards it, therefore, the minds of the moralists of our age should turn; even should they judge it to be incomplete, it must nevertheless be adopted as necessary.[34]

What makes its adoption necessary is the fact that the possibility of successfully appealing to the inherent attractiveness of virtue has vanished with the destruction of the feudal system, and with it the belief in authority and the dignity of nonmaterial ends. Tocqueville is willing to concede that even in aristocratic times, men acted more often than not from less than altruistic motives; but it was important to the system that appeals in the name of disinterested virtue might still be made without embarrassment.[f] Such appeals are impossible in the democratic world: given the flux and uncertainty surrounding all opinions, "Men cling to the mere instincts and material interests of their position, which are naturally more tangible, definite, and permanent than any opinions in the world."[35] Since equality of conditions supports the attack of individualism on all the traditional sources of morality, private interest becomes the principal if not the only spring of human action. Private interest, Tocqueville affirms, is "the only immutable point in the human heart." And "if, in the midst of this general disruption, you do not succeed in connecting the idea of rights with that of private interest . . . what means will you have of governing the world except by fear?"[36] Tocqueville's reference to "connecting" the idea of rights (which he considers "simply that of virtue introduced into the political world"[37]) with that of private interest is ambiguous: it may refer to either a theoretical or a rhetorical connection. Tocqueville intends both interpretations: it is incumbent on the teachers and moralists of the present to both regard and preach the unity of the two ideas as the last remaining hope for the resuscitation of public virtue. The union of the two ideas is the doctrine of self-interest rightly understood.

How is the concept of self-interest modified by the requirement that it be understood *rightly?* Is self-interest

---

[f] Cf. Tocqueville, *Democracy*, II, 129: "I doubt whether men were more virtuous in aristocratic ages than in others, but they were incessantly talking of the beauties of virtue, and its utility was only studied in secret."

rightly understood equivalent to the pursuit of one's true interest? If so, what is a man's true interest?[38] Every philosophic attempt to explain man's nature and his place in the universe as a whole might be offered in answer. It would be difficult to prove that any of them lie outside Tocqueville's purview, but it is nevertheless true that within the context of his concern with democracy, self-interest is understood primarily in an economic sense—it is identified with the most immediate, tangible, material signs of a man's well-being.[g] Out of an enlightened regard for one's own material welfare, and the intelligent pursuit of it, a good other than an economic one emerges: patriotism or public-spiritedness.

Still, a man may pursue even his material interests under differing moral perspectives. He may be persuaded, for example, of the truth of Mandeville's maxim that private vices lead to public benefits, and hence that nothing more is required of him than total concentration on maximizing his immediate gains. This idea Tocqueville considers especially reprehensible; to counter it he offers his own doctrine. Contrasting his doctrine with the idea that man serves his fellow creatures best in serving himself, he laments: "Everybody I see about me seems bent on teaching his contemporaries, by precept and example, that what is useful is never wrong. Will nobody undertake to make them understand how what is right may be useful?"[39] Both ideas ap-

---

[g] There are, of course, exceptions, which point to self-preservation as the ultimate self-interest. See, e.g., Tocqueville's discussion of the plight of the southern plantation owner (*Democracy*, I, 394–95): "Not that the inhabitants of the South regard slavery as necessary to the wealth of the planter; on this point many of them agree with their Northern countrymen in freely admitting that slavery is prejudicial to their interests; but they are convinced that the removal of this evil would imperil their own existence . . . . Hence arises a singular contrast: the more the utility of slavery is contested, the more firmly is it established in the laws." In this case, at least, Tocqueville does not affirm that reliance on interest in the economic sense is the best course; short of a disastrous civil war, the problem appears virtually insoluble to him.

peal, ultimately, to the self-regarding instincts of man, but Mandeville's makes no provision for the emergence of political virtues: it would only intensify the modern tendency toward individualism. If men are not to withdraw entirely into their own domestic circles, if public-spiritedness is not to disappear altogether, men must be taught that out of an enlightened regard for themselves they constantly need to assist one another, and to sacrifice some portion of their time and wealth to the welfare of the state or community. Men must come to see the desirability of postponing the immediate gratification of their desires, in the expectation of greater or more certain satisfaction to arise from the contribution of the common welfare to their own well-being. The foundation of the public or social order rests on enlightened selfishness: each individual accepts the view that "man serves himself in serving his fellow creatures. . . . His private interest is to do good."[40] Faithful to the requirements of equality, Tocqueville strives to evolve a species of public morality and patriotism out of the self-regarding instincts of man: he would indeed make men virtuous by teaching them that what is right is also useful.

Self-interest is a doctrine that may be thoroughly relied on:

The principle of self-interest rightly understood is not a lofty one, but it is clear and sure. It does not aim at mighty objects, but attains without exertion all those at which it aims. As it lies within the reach of all capacities, everyone can without difficulty learn and retain it. By its admirable conformity to human weaknesses it easily obtains great dominion; nor is that dominion precarious, since the principle checks one personal interest by another, and uses, to direct the passions, the very same instrument that excites them.[41]

This succinct statement reveals Tocqueville's fundamental agreement with the presuppositions of modern political thought; despite apparent departures, he follows in the tradition originating with Machiavelli and continuing in the natural-rights teaching of Hobbes. The political problem of man is solved by lowering one's standards—the doctrine of self-interest rightly understood does not aim at lofty objects. The realization of what standards are adopted is ensured by relying on a doctrine within the reach of the meanest capacity, hence within the reach of all. The doctrine has its roots in what is considered to be man's most powerful passion—here, his concern for his own well-being. The success of the doctrine is still further guaranteed by playing one interest off against another while turning over to reason the office of ensuring the satisfaction of the passions. "In man," Tocqueville tells us, "the angel teaches the brute the art of satisfying its desires."[h] In the manner of modern political philosophy, Tocqueville makes use of what is operative in most men most of the time; not unexpectedly, this turns out to be their lowest rather than their highest motive. As in Machiavelli, the primary consideration is what men are, not what they may become. It is interesting that Tocqueville could write the following to his friend Kergolay at precisely the time he had been reading the works of Machiavelli:

Whatever we do we cannot prevent men from having a body as well as a soul, as if an angel occupied the form of an animal. . . . A system of philosophy or of religion that chooses entirely to ignore the one or the other may produce some extraordinary cases, but will never exercise any general influence over mankind: this I believe and deplore, for you know that though the animal is not more subdued in me than in most people, I adore the angel, and would give anything to make it predominate. I

---

[h] Tocqueville, *Democracy*, II, 157. Cf. Hobbes, p. 46: "For the thoughts are to the desires as scouts and spies, to range abroad and find the way to the things desired."

am, therefore, continually at work to discover a middle course which men may follow without becoming disciples either of Heliogabalus or of St. Jerome; for I am convinced that the great majority will never be persuaded to imitate either, and less the saint than the emperor. I am, then, not so much shocked as you are by the *decorous materialism* of which you complain so bitterly; not that it does not excite my contempt as much as it does yours; but I consider it practically, and I ask myself whether if not exactly this, something like it be not, in fact, all that one can expect, not of any particular man, but of the species in general.[i]

Tocqueville is no Philistine; he is not insensitive to what is highest in man. He could be contemptuous of the "discreet, well-regulated sensualism" arising from the craving for material well-being.[42] Between the so-called civic or bourgeois virtues and the extraordinary virtues—artistry, heroism, valor, glory, and magnanimity—there was no contest. Yet the doctrine he urges encourages the whole range of bourgeois virtues, and makes barely any provision for the emergence of the more exalted ones.

The principle of self-interest rightly understood produces no great acts of self-sacrifice, but it suggests daily small acts of self-denial. By itself it cannot suffice to make a man virtuous; but it disciplines a number of persons in habits of regularity, temperance, moderation, foresight, self-command; and if it does not lead men [to will themselves] straight to virtue . . . it gradually draws them in that direction by their habits. If the principle of self-interest rightly understood were to sway the whole moral world, extraordinary virtues would doubtless be more rare; but I think that gross depravity would then also be less common. The principle of interest rightly understood perhaps prevents men from rising far above the level of mankind, but a great number

---

[i] Tocqueville to Kergolay, August 5, 1836, *Memoir*, I, 304–5. From the passages following these, it is clear that Tocqueville does not agree with Machiavelli in all respects, perhaps not even in the most important (i.e., about the status of the moral order).

of other men, who were falling far below it, are caught and re-strained by it. Observe some few individuals, they are lowered by it; survey mankind, [it is] raised.*ʲ*

In an age in which everything conspires to make a man think only of himself, the only virtues possible are those fostered by the doctrine of self-interest rightly understood. Should no attempt be made to teach men how to under-stand their true interests, "It is difficult to foresee to what pitch of stupid excesses their selfishness may lead them; and no one can foretell into what disgrace and wretchedness they would plunge themselves lest they should have to sacrifice something of their own well-being to the prosperity of their fellow creatures."[43]

It is not surprising, of course, that the sense of public virtue the new doctrine fosters bears unmistakable signs of its influence. Originating in calculation and egoism, this sense of virtue is itself rational and interested. The goal of a selfless devotion to country is abandoned. In former times, patriotism had more of a religious fervor; men acted more from belief than from calculation. They were, per-haps, more generous and more ardent—but no purpose is served by being nostalgic: "To retreat is impossible, for a people cannot recover the sentiments of their youth. . . . They must go forward and accelerate the union of private with public interests, since the period of disinterested patri-otism is gone . . . forever."[44]

It is disconcerting to realize that Tocqueville seems ob-livious to the possibility of some irreconcilable conflict be-

---

ʲ Tocqueville, *Democracy*, II, 131. On the use of self-interest rightly under-stood, Doris Goldstein comments: "This 'middle road' in morality, in Tocque-ville's judgment certainly not the highest or the noblest, was suitable to a demo-cratic age just because most men could follow it. After all, 'most men,' or the majority, would govern in a democracy; therefore it was necessary to find some guiding principle which would insure the existence of public morality." ("Tocque-ville's Concept of Citizenship," p. 52.)

tween public and private interest. He does not even consider whether men are as well equipped to deal with the
common good as they are with their own, nor what will
happen when the common good requires at least a temporary sacrifice by each citizen. It is instructive to compare
the differences in approach between Rousseau and Tocqueville on this issue. Rousseau begins the *Social Contract* by
explicitly committing himself, in fulfilling his objective, to
uniting right with interest, "in order that justice and utility
may in no case be divided."[45] But in the passage already
quoted, in which he calls for the virtual annihilation of the
individual and his interest, Rousseau implicitly recognizes
the impossibility of uniting the public and the private.[46]
One is left wondering if the political problem of man can
be resolved on the basis of an alleged harmony between
public and private interests. Tocqueville, however, scarcely
allows any such speculation to make its appearance in the
Democracy. It, like all his works, is meant to be hortatory:
to encumber it with doubts would only weaken its effectiveness. However, doubts do appear in the notes he wrote
while in America: "To what degree can these two principles of private and public welfare be blended? To what
point can a conscience born of reflection and calculation
overcome political passions not yet visible, but which cannot help arising? Only the future will show us."[47] Moreover, even within the *Democracy* Tocqueville indirectly admits to some doubts by questioning the genuineness of the
devotion to the common good that arises from enlightened
self-interest:

The inhabitants of the United States talk much of their attachment to their country; but I confess that I do not rely upon that
calculating patriotism which is founded upon interest, and which
a change in the interest may destroy. . . . A government retains
its sway over a great number of citizens far less by the voluntary

and rational consent of the multitude than by that instinctive and to a certain extent involuntary agreement which results from similarity of feelings and resemblances of opinion.[k]

It is ostensibly to remedy the deficiencies of the doctrine of self-interest rightly understood, and to provide for "those opinions and sentiments that may be termed the immaterial interests of men,"[48] that Tocqueville turns to religion. In so doing, he follows in a long tradition. Almost without exception, the founders of our nation began the American experiment firmly convinced that its success was partly dependent on the support of religion. They welcomed religious support from any source: the major documents of our beginnings refer alike to revealed religion and to rational theology. The reason for their concern was in all cases the same—the belief that the moral foundations of democracy required otherworldly buttressing. Both of Washington's principal addresses to the American people illustrate this persistent theme. His inaugural address proclaims the "indissoluble union between virtue and happiness," and cautions that "we ought to be no less persuaded that the propitious smiles of Heaven can never be expected on a nation that disregards the eternal rules of order and right, which Heaven itself has ordained." At the close of his administration, he warns: "Let us with caution indulge the supposition that morality can be maintained without religion. Whatever may be conceded to the influence of refined education on minds of peculiar structure, reason and experience both forbid us to expect that National morality can prevail in exclusion of religious principle."[49]

That religion may subserve political purposes was hardly a new idea; moreover, nondemocratic regimes were not the

[k] Tocqueville, *Democracy*, I, 408–9. The original is even stronger: "J'avoue que je ne me fie point..." (I confess that I do not rely *at all*...), *Oeuvres Complètes* (Mayer), I, Part 1, 389.

only ones traditionally thought to require religious support. In the modern age, as traditional religious institutions grew weaker and the liberal tradition took shape, a view arose that democracy could dispense with religious support; in fact, that religion and freedom were incompatible.[50] The one was a manifestation of man's finitude and ultimate dependence, the other an assertion of his creativity and absolute independence. Rousseau rejected this alleged dichotomy, and sought to preserve both religion and freedom by transforming religion itself into a product of man's creativity. He called for the creation of a civil religion whose simple dogmas must be observed by all free citizens. The man who did not believe, or acted as if he did not believe, would be branded as an "anti-social being, incapable of truly loving the laws and justice, and of sacrificing, at need, his life to his duty."[51] The citizens of Rousseau's free republic, aware of the need to restrain their appetites and whims, will in their capacity as sovereign impose religious dogmas upon themselves, and in extreme cases will punish violators of those dogmas by death. Rousseau thus rejects traditional religion while preserving its utilitarian function.

Tocqueville saw in Rousseau's formulation the dilemma of democracy, at least as it had come to be understood since the eighteenth century: if men are to be free, they must not be subject to any restraints; yet freedom cannot be guaranteed without restraints that, if they are not to violate the spirit of freedom, must be self-imposed. But self-imposed restraints are self-removable, and hence are no restraints at all. Few men have thought about the problem of democracy, and religion's role in it, as deeply as Tocqueville. He realized that the Americans had combined the spirit of liberty with that of religion, and he sought to elicit from their experience the principle that would resolve Rousseau's dilemma. Tocqueville was convinced that however necessary religion was to a well-ordered democracy, it could not successfully rely on being freely accepted by the citizens themselves.

At first sight, Tocqueville's insistence on the indispensability of religion appears to indicate a serious deficiency in the doctrine of self-interest rightly understood. That the chapter on self-interest in the *Democracy* is followed immediately by one calling attention to the limitations of the doctrine reinforces this impression. "Whatever ingenuity may be put forth to demonstrate the utility of virtue, it will never be an easy task to make that man live aright who does not wish to die."[52] But the second chapter does not dwell on the shortcomings of self-interest—its real purpose is to show how a species of religious feeling may be generated by judiciously applying the doctrine itself.

As ordinarily understood, the doctrine prescribes that one deny the impulse to gratify one's desires immediately in return for a greater or more intense pleasure in the future. In this way one can encourage citizens to fulfill their day-to-day obligations to the state, take part in elections, serve on juries, and the like. But the safety or well-being of the nation may sometimes demand sacrifices for which men cannot reasonably expect any reward in this life. How can such demands be justified? Moreover, what about those who cannot be convinced that they have more to gain by temporarily sacrificing their immediate interest than by relentlessly pursuing it? Tocqueville's reply is hardly original: virtue must have an otherworldly support. What may be novel, though, is his suggestion that such support may be gained simply by extending the doctrine of self-interest to include the rewards of a future life. Tocqueville contends that the founders of almost all religions have used the same language in advancing their causes that moral philosophers have used in setting forth the principle of self-interest: the way is the same, "only the goal is more remote." He does not deny that some holy men may have acted entirely out of love of God, but he insists that "self-interest is the principal means that religions themselves employ to govern men. . . . In this way they strike the multitude and become popular."[53]

Tocqueville strikes a utilitarian attitude toward religion throughout. He invokes it not only to justify sacrifice that cannot be rewarded in this world, but also to combat both the individualism and materialism democracy produces. Religion shows men that there are goals and aspirations that transcend the experience of their senses; it thus combats the materialist teaching that everything is reducible to matter and that man's spirit perishes with the body. It awakens men's "sublimest faculties" and puts them to use; moreover, it reminds men of their obligations to one another, and by so doing reduces their preoccupation with themselves. It is religion that renders freedom salutary: freedom is impossible without morality, and morality impossible without religion.[54]

Despotism may govern without faith, but liberty cannot. Religion . . . is more needed in democratic republics than in any others. How is it possible that society should escape destruction if the moral tie is not strengthened in proportion as the political tie is relaxed? And what can be done with a people who are their own masters if they are not submissive to the Deity?[1]

---

[1] Tocqueville, *Democracy*, I, 318. Cf. Bryce: "The more democratic republics become, the more the masses grow conscious of their own power, the more do they need to live, not only by patriotism, but by reverence and self-control, and the more essential to their well-being are those sources whence reverence and self-control flow." This particular passage is cited in Lowenthal's "Van Alstyne on the Establishment of Religion," p. 394. Lowenthal's entire article should be consulted for a contemporary restatement of the problem of religion in a democracy. He contends that "a society stressing individual rights and individual self-care is in need of a balancing stress on duties and human brotherhood, and this element is best supplied not by the teaching of the Declaration but by our Biblical religious tradition." (*Ibid.*)

Religion's utility is not solely negative. It not only restrains man; by supplying the "dogmatic beliefs" that are the cement of society, it overcomes the atomization of democracy and makes possible political life, in the sense of the activity of men drawn together by common values. Thus Tocqueville's defense of religious belief may be seen as the conclusion of a complex demonstration of the necessity for dogmatic beliefs, or principles of authority. The argument is familiar to anyone who has ever reflected on the vast number of things he must accept on faith in order to do anything—say, to leave home and go to work. He must assume the existence and persistence without radical change of the objects outside him and the laws by which they function; he may utilize, without comprehending, means of transportation that result from very sophisticated applications of those laws; and so forth. Man is always "reduced to take on trust a host of facts and opinions which he has not had either the time or the power to verify for himself, but which men of greater ability have found out, or which the crowd adopts." This is no less true of philosophers than it is of ordinary men: "There is no philosopher in the world so great but that he believes a million things on the faith of other people and accepts a great many more truths than he demonstrates."[55] Society too is dependent on beliefs that are taken on faith, beliefs that all its citizens must hold in common:

Without such common belief no society can prosper; say, rather, no society can exist; for without ideas held in common there is no common action, and without common action there may still be men, but there is no social body. . . . The minds of all the citizens should be rallied and held together by certain predominant ideas; and this cannot be the case unless each of them sometimes draws his opinions from the common source and consents to accept certain matters of belief already formed.[56]

Tocqueville is not concerned with just any dogmatic belief, but with the central one that occasions virtually all human activity:

There is hardly any human action, however particular it may be, that does not originate in some very general idea men have conceived of the Deity, of his relation to mankind, of the nature of their own souls, and of their duties to their fellow creatures. Nor can anything prevent these ideas from being the common spring from which all the rest emanate.[57]

Without firm beliefs about God and human nature men may quickly be reduced to "disorder and impotence," especially in times of extreme individualism, when opinions about these fundamentals are so varied and changeable that they undermine each man's confidence in his own beliefs. Mental and spiritual paralysis may then ensue, exposing every man to the subtle allure of the first demagogue to promise order and stability. Firm beliefs about God and nature are therefore necessary for human freedom, at least for political freedom.[m] Paradoxically, the price of this freedom is the freedom to inquire into the very basis of our beliefs: "General ideas respecting God and human nature are . . . the ideas above all others which it is most suitable to withdraw from the habitual action of private judgment and in which there is most to gain and least to lose by recognizing a principle of authority."[58]

Toqueville argues that "none but minds singularly free from the ordinary cares of life, minds at once penetrating, subtle, and trained by thinking can, even with much time and care, sound the depths of these truths [about God and man's nature]."[59] But he does not set such minds to formu-

---

[m] As Jefferson put it (II, 227): "Can the liberties of a nation be thought secure when we have removed their only firm basis, a conviction in the minds of the people that these liberties are the gift of God? That they are not to be violated but with His wrath?"

lating beliefs about the basic philosophical questions, for after two thousand years philosophers have left us nothing but conflicting notions. What is apparently beyond their capacity to settle is clearly beyond most other men; if not beyond their intellectual capacity, then beyond the resources of time and leisure at their disposal. During his trip to America, Tocqueville had expressed to Channing, the distinguished Unitarian minister, his fear of "the distance that the human spirit [had] traveled since Catholicism." A few more steps would lead to a kind of natural religion beyond the capacity of the average man, leaving him without any belief at all. Tocqueville asked Channing:

Do you not think that human nature is so constituted that, whatever the improvements in education and the state of society, there will always be found a great mass of men who are incapable from the nature of their position of setting their reason to work on theoretical and abstract questions, and who, if they do not have a dogmatic faith, will not exactly believe in anything?[60]

Channing's reply, that religious questions were in fact not beyond the capacity of any man, failed to reassure Tocqueville. The questions seemed to him too subtle, too complex; man's understanding, too limited.

If men cannot determine for themselves the answers to the eternal questions; if philosophers cannot agree; and if it is nevertheless essential to the freedom, the unity, and the well-being of society that there be a commonly held core of such beliefs—then society must have recourse to religious dogma to supply that core. "Of all the kinds of dogmatic belief, the most desirable appears to me to be dogmatic belief in matters of religion; and this is a clear inference, even from no higher consideration than the interests of this world." About the role of religion, there is no ambiguity:

The first object and one of the principal advantages of religion is to furnish to each of these fundamental questions a solution that to the mass of mankind is at once clear, precise, intelligible, and lasting. There are religions that are false and very absurd, but it may be affirmed that any religion which remains within the circle I have just traced . . . imposes a salutary restraint on the intellect; and it must be admitted that, if it does not save men in another world, it is at least very conducive to their happiness and their greatness in this.[61]

Although Tocqueville alludes to "false and very absurd" religions, he is virtually indifferent to the particular tenets of the religion professed by this or that democratic society. He does not defend the withdrawal of the right to inquire into fundamental beliefs by insisting on the need to preserve revealed truths. "If it be of the highest importance to man, as an individual, that his religion be true, it is not so to society. Society has no future life to hope for or to fear . . . provided the citizens profess a religion, the peculiar tenets of that religion are of little importance to its interests." However sincere a Christian Tocqueville himself may have been, he conceived of *Democracy in America* as a political treatise; and in it, as in all his political writings, he considers religion with an eye to its political utility.[n]

Tocqueville's defense of the utility of religion does not lead him to advocate a state religion; on the contrary, political considerations force him to the conclusion that the separation of church and state is necessary. But unlike those

[n] Tocqueville, *Democracy*, I, 314. Cf. Rousseau, pp. 138–39: "It matters very much to the community that each citizen should have a religion. That will make him love his duty; but the dogmas of that religion concern the State and its members only so far as they have reference to morality and to the duties which he who professes them is bound to do to others." For supporting interpretations of Tocqueville's use and understanding of religion, see Lively, pp. 37–38, 197–99; Drescher, pp. 11–13. According to Redier (p. 55): "[Tocqueville] said, 'I am an unbeliever,' and courted the faithful. He was clearly interested in religion as a means, not an end. His objective was politics, a politics of free men; his means was Roman Catholicism, with its dogmas and its discipline." For opposing ideas on Tocqueville and religion, see Goldstein, "Religious Beliefs of Alexis de Tocqueville," pp. 379–93, especially pp. 385, 387; Nef, pp. 460–82; and Wach, pp. 74–90, especially pp. 77, 79.

who sought to strengthen the political order while weakening the religious, Tocqueville argues that religion can remain strong enough to influence a democratic society only if it stays clear of politics; entering into them will inevitably suggest that religious tenets are subject to majority determination.° The settlers of New England had bequeathed to their descendants the precious knowledge of how the spirit of liberty and the spirit of religion could be combined. Man's search for solutions to political problems is unremitting and uninhibited, but "having reached the limits of the political world, the human spirit stops of itself; in fear it relinquishes the need of exploration; it even abstains from lifting the veil of the sanctuary; it bows with respect before truths which it accepts without discussion."[62] Democracy, it seems, is impossible without such a sanctuary above and beyond democratic inquiry; and all of Tocqueville's efforts are bent on preserving this sanctuary from the impious and destructive onslaughts of the many. This is a delicate enterprise, one requiring that innovation be avoided at all costs. Men should conserve what religious tastes already exist; unlike Rousseau, they should not even consider constructing religious or civil dogmas. "When, therefore, *any* religion has struck its roots deep into a democracy, beware that you do not disturb it; but rather watch it carefully, as the most precious bequest of aristocratic ages. Do not seek to supersede the old religious opinions of men by new ones."ᵖ Re-

---

° "[Edward VI's] reign delightfully proves how men need *authority* in questions of religion, and how far they go astray when they lose a sure basis and appeal to their reason alone. One finds them then discussing various questions of belief as if they were so many paragraphs in a Bill, and a simple majority would decide what was or was not so in spiritual matters, determining what one must believe or answer to be saved in the next world and not to be hanged in this." (Tocqueville, *Journey to England and Ireland*, p. 40; see also p. 64; *Democracy*, I, 320–26.)

ᵖ Tocqueville, *Democracy*, II, 154–55, italics mine. If religious beliefs have already weakened, Tocqueville advises governments to encourage their restoration by inspiring citizens with long-term projects: "I do not doubt that by training the members of a community to think of their future condition in this world,

membering Hobbes's maxim that the examples of princes are more persuasive than the laws themselves, Tocqueville asserts that "the sole effectual means which governments can employ in order to have the doctrine of the immortality of the soul duly respected is always to act as if they believed in it themselves."[63]

Tocqueville is aware that equality of conditions imposes limitations on religion. If religion is to remain faithful to its political function, it must accept these limitations; it too must be consonant with the principle of democratic regimes. It must defer, without surrendering, to the passions unleashed by equality. For example, it cannot hope to persuade men that the passion for self-gratification is immoral, but it may try to moderate and regulate their drive for well-being.[64] It must hold fast to the fundamentals of its creed, but must not excite the hostility of the majority by needless opposition "to the ideas that generally prevail or to the permanent interests that exist in the mass of the people. . . . By respecting all democratic tendencies not absolutely contrary to herself, and by making use of several of them for her own purposes, religion sustains a successful struggle with that spirit of individual independence which is her most dangerous opponent."[q]

Save for an occasional tone of deep conviction, Tocque-

---

they would be gradually and unconsciously brought nearer to religious convictions. Thus the means that allow men, up to a certain point, to go without religion are perhaps, after all, the only means we still possess for bringing mankind back, by a long and roundabout path, to a state of faith." (*Ibid.*, p. 160.)

[q] Tocqueville, *Democracy*, II, 28–29. As an example of the value to religion of respecting democratic tendencies, Tocqueville describes how American clergymen admit to their parishioners that an honest concern for the material comforts of this world need not be antithetical to their hopes for eternal happiness. As a result, "Public opinion is never hostile to [the clergy]; it rather supports and protects them." Tocqueville also argues *ad hominem*: he would have men moderate their pursuit of well-being by realizing that the exclusive pursuit of it lowers and enervates the soul, and that a strong soul will be more successful in pursuing well-being than a weak one. (*Ibid.*, p. 157.)

ville's treatment of religion is one of unrelieved functionalism. Apparently he believes religion to be compatible with almost any democratic tendency. Its practices are flexible: since democratic man abjures forms and symbols, religious ones are to be restricted to an absolute minimum. Its tenets are flexible too; many usually associated with religions may be completely forgone. Democratic man need not believe in an afterlife of reward and punishment, or even, in fact, in an undying human soul. Tocqueville expresses no preference for any particular doctrine: he thinks of most religions as "only general, simple, and practical means of teaching men the doctrine of the immortality of the soul."[65] But the following passage makes it clear that "the immortality of the soul" does not mean the specific immutability of the *human* soul:

The doctrine of metempsychosis is assuredly not more rational than that of materialism; nevertheless, if it were absolutely necessary that a democracy should choose one of the two, I should not hesitate to decide that the community would run less risk of being brutalized by believing that the soul of man will pass into the carcass of a hog than by believing that the soul of man is nothing at all. The belief in a supersensual and immortal principle, united for a time to matter, is so indispensable to man's greatness that its effects are striking *even when it is not united to the doctrine of future reward and punishment*, or even when it teaches no more than that *after death the divine principle contained in man is absorbed in the Deity or transferred to animate the frame of some other creature.*[66]

That Tocqueville should resort to so extreme a statement indicates that his primary concern with religion was not with the support it might give morality by promises of rewards or punishments in an afterlife, but rather with the support it would inevitably give a people's sense of continuity and futurity, without which there could be no thought of greatness. There were forces at work within democracy that offered hope that its citizens would not be without the ordinary decencies—they would be good fathers, honest merchants, diligent providers, etc.—but without a conviction that the efforts of one generation would be preserved and completed by those of the next no heroic tasks would even be contemplated, let alone undertaken. Tocqueville relied on religion to supply this conviction, for "religions give men a general habit of conducting themselves with a view to eternity; in this respect [religions] are not less useful to happiness in this life than to felicity hereafter, and this is one of their chief political characteristics."[r]

But how will a religion pared down to simple and uniform generalizations about God and human nature, a religion that must continually defer to democratic passions, a religion that derives its strength not from divine revelation, but from majority agreement, be able to mold and restrain the democratic majority itself?[s] The answer is

[r] Tocqueville, *Democracy*, II, 158–60. Bryce has captured Tocqueville's intent exactly: "There has never been a civilized nation without a religion, and though many highly civilized individual men live without it, they are obviously the children of a state of sentiment and thought in which religion has been a powerful factor. . . . No one can conjecture what a race of men would be like who during several generations believed themselves to be the highest beings in the universe, or at least entirely out of relation to any other higher beings, and to be therewithal destined to no kind of existence after death. . . . All that need be here said is that a people with comparatively little around it in the way of historic memories and associations to touch its emotion, a people whose energy is chiefly absorbed in commerce and the development of the material resources of its territory, a people consumed by a feverish activity that gives little opportunity for reflection or for the contemplation of nature, seems most of all to need to have its horizon widened, its sense of awe and mystery touched, by whatever calls it away from the busy world of sight and sound into the stillness of faith and meditation." (*Commonwealth*, II, 495–96.)

[s] Tocqueville's recognition that religion in a democracy could have no other basis than majority agreement is clear: "Religion itself holds sway [in America] much less as a doctrine of revelation than as a commonly received opinion." That this is true is due to the operation of the principle of equality itself; hence, the fact is not peculiar to America per se. Moreover, "It may be foreseen that faith in public opinion will become for [democratic men] a species of religion, and the majority its ministering prophet." (*Democracy*, II, 12.)

simple: it will not. We are told that the well-being of society depends on religion; but religion is equally dependent on society. For a religion to be effective at all, its adherents must have a faith resistant to temporal stresses and strains. If that faith has no support but majority opinion, it must inevitably decay. Leroy, agreeing that "it was a fantasy to imagine that religion would remain by its permanence the immovable regulator of the moving spirit of democratic liberty," quotes Eugène d'Eichthal's telling comment: "To exhort a people to believe, is that not to suppose that they will believe what they wish?"[67] In fact, Tocqueville encourages such criticism by considering religion from solely a "human point of view." The concessions he recommends making to democratic propensities so that religion may retain its power threaten to undermine religion altogether. He does not undertake a defense of religion—not, that is, of true religion, or even of religion as it was traditionally understood. Instead, he concentrates first on identifying the features of any religion (or of anything passing for religion) that are consonant with the needs of society, and then on trying to discover ways of preserving those features from the attacks of skepticism.[t]

[t] Cf. Tocqueville, *Democracy*, II, 23–24: "I have neither the right nor the intention of examining the supernatural means that God employs to infuse religious belief into the heart of man. I am at this moment considering religions in a purely human point of view; my object is to inquire by what means they may most easily retain their sway in the democratic ages upon which we are entering."

Doris Goldstein, in her excellent monograph, "Tocqueville's Concept of Citizenship," argues that Tocqueville *was* concerned with genuine religion, and with the need to reconcile its requirements with those of a modern egalitarian society. She calls attention (pp. 50–51) to Tocqueville's unequivocal statement that belief in the Gospels was the source of all public or private morality. Yet it is difficult if not impossible to reconcile her theory with his oft-expressed opinion that any religion would do. Moreover, in the *Democracy* he traces the source of all values to the fundamental wants and needs of men as men; that is, he gives an entirely secular account of morality. Another passage (I, 320–21) may be thought to be a consideration of true religion: "The short space of threescore years can never content the imagination of man; nor can the imperfect joys of this world satisfy his heart. Man alone, of all created beings, displays a natural

As we have seen, Tocqueville is virtually indifferent to the dogma this or that society adopts or adheres to. What he recommends to ensure the well-being of democratic regimes is little more than the propagation of spiritualistic myths designed to satisfy and put to use the human soul's demand for some answer to the question of immortality. Propagating such salutary myths cannot but weaken genuine religious belief rather than strengthening it, for by propagating them men are emboldened to consider religion from a functional point of view. But there is no assurance that genuine religion is necessarily salutary, and in case of conflict, society will surely sacrifice the genuine for the salutary. Moreover, the effectiveness of spiritualistic myths is dependent on whether their nature remains hidden; they are not likely to retain their usefulness if they are known to be myths. It is doubtful whether any amount of self-interest rightly understood can not only induce a man to act for a long period of time as if myths of his own devising had some transcendental origin, but can finally manage to persuade him that his pretense is the truth. As Engels said, in another context: "That the material life conditions of the persons inside whose heads this thought process goes on in

---

contempt of existence, and yet a boundless desire to exist; he scorns life, but he dreads annihilation. These different feelings incessantly urge his soul to the contemplation of a future state, and religion directs his musings thither. Religion, then, is simply another form of hope, and it is no less natural to the human heart than hope itself. Men cannot abandon their religious faith without a kind of aberration of intellect and a sort of violent distortion of their true nature; they are invincibly brought back to more pious sentiments. Unbelief is an accident, and faith is the only permanent state of mankind. If we consider religious institutions merely in a human point of view, they may be said to derive an inexhaustible element of strength from man himself, since they belong to one of the constituent principles of human nature." The same idea is also set forth in his *European Revolution* (pp. 170–71*n*). The important point, however, is that he is still considering religion from a human point of view. Religion may derive its permanence from a fundamental need of human nature, but there is no reason not to believe that one religion will satisfy the soul as well as another, or even that gross superstition will satisfy as well as genuine revelation. Cf. Hobbes, pp. 70, 77.

the last resort determine the course of this process *remains of necessity unknown to these persons,* for otherwise there would be an end to all ideology."[68]

If spiritualistic myths cannot resolve the problem of democracy, what of genuine religion? Unfortunately for the prospects of a solution, a genuine religion must transcend society: it must be the ultimate sovereign of the men who believe in it. Such a religion cannot be the projection of a secular society, in the words of a modern writer, but must determine the nature of society "from a point of reference beyond it."[69] Democratic society, however, is synonymous with the sovereignty of the people. I suggest that Tocqueville, considering the irreconcilable demands of genuine religion and the democratic principle of equality, abandoned the one in order to save the other. To have done otherwise would have meant abandoning the quest to resolve the problem of democracy on the level of democracy itself.

If Tocqueville's analysis is correct, and democracy cannot achieve greatness without a morality that draws its strength from religion, and if my analysis is also correct, and neither genuine religion nor spiritualistic myth can retain its power in a democracy, we are forced to question Tocqueville's success in evolving restraints on the democratic tendencies toward materialism and mediocrity. Of course, it may be that Tocqueville's belief in the indispensability of religious restraints is unfounded. Man's comprehension of the overriding importance of the general welfare, and his ability to make sacrifices for it, may be greater than Tocqueville would allow. It may also be that my analysis is defective in that it underestimates man's capacity to persist in a delusion, a capacity that may very well sustain spiritualistic myths.

Tocqueville, like some others, could have sought an alternative to religion—a substitute that was free from the defects of religion, but would fulfill the functions of faith. In fact, he experimented with just such a substitute in encouraging the spirit of commerce—the spirit, that is, of the pursuit of well-being rightly understood. This seems paradoxical, considering Tocqueville's criticism of a society wholly given over to the pursuit of well-being. But I believe that Tocqueville's criticism has been exaggerated. That he valued the goods of the soul over those of the body has been amply demonstrated, but that he scorned all materialism, or that material goods stood beneath his contempt,[u] is less evident. I believe that there is evidence to support quite a contrary opinion.

At the beginning of the *Democracy* is a brief account (to which Tocqueville later returns) of the people who inhabited America before the colonists. The Indians occupy an anomalous role in human history, for though they were free, equal, and religious—the main characteristics of the democratic men who were to play the major role in the ages about to unfold—they were nevertheless destined to make room for others. Their virtues as well as their vices contributed to their downfall. In general, they "were ignorant of the value of riches, and indifferent to the enjoyments that civilized man procures for himself by their means."[70] Being hunters, they occupied the land without appropriating or cultivating it, an "indispensable preliminary to civilization." Above all, they considered labor "not merely as an evil, but as a disgrace." This "ancient prejudice" was shared by the noblemen of the Middle Ages; and it is perhaps no accident that both Indians and nobles fell victims to a commercial society.[71] The Indians seemed to Tocqueville "to have been placed by Providence amid the riches of the New World only to enjoy them for a season. . . . Those coasts, so

---

[u] As has been suggested by Goldstein ("Religious Beliefs of Tocqueville," p. 381) and Pierson (p. 63).

admirably adapted for commerce and industry; those wide
and deep rivers; that inexhaustible valley of the Missis-
sippi; the whole continent, in short, seemed prepared to
be the abode of a great nation yet unborn."[72]

Tocqueville thought of the quest for well-being as an
"honest and lawful pursuit," even if it did not exhaust
man's potentialities.[73] Actually, this pursuit was more important to him than might be suggested by the phrase "honest and lawful." Consider, for example, the following:

> If I had been born in an aristocratic age, in the midst of a nation
> where the hereditary wealth of some and the irremediable penury
> of others equally diverted men from the idea of bettering their
> condition and held the soul, as it were, in a state of torpor, fixed
> on the contemplation of another world, I should then wish that
> it were possible for me to rouse that people to a sense of their
> wants; I should seek to discover more rapid and easy means for
> satisfying the fresh desires that I might have awakened; and,
> directing the most strenuous efforts of the citizens to physical
> pursuits, I should endeavor to stimulate them to promote their
> own well-being.[74]

That he would have been prepared to divert men's concern
from their eternal to their immediate well-being does not
imply that he valued the goods of this world above those
of the next; but it does tend to support the idea that he was
not contemptuous of material progress.

Of course, he could approve of men's seeking a modest
improvement in their material welfare and still be critical
of an unrestrained quest for material goods. The clue to his
attitude toward unrestrained acquisitiveness, I believe, is
his evaluation of the theories that purported to explain the
new growth of commercial spirit in the seventeenth and
eighteenth centuries. A very perceptive study of Tocqueville's grasp of both the principles and consequences of the
new economic theories is made by Seymour Drescher in his

Tocqueville and England.[75] Drescher shows that Tocqueville's acquaintance with laissez-faire economic theory is secondhand, and his interest in it perfunctory—compared, at least, to his passion for political matters. Nevertheless, Tocqueville called his readers' attention to the "new axioms of the science of manufactures" and to the "great principle of political economy"; moreover, he admitted to Lord Radnor that "the truth of the principles [of political economy] is incontestable."[v] His adherence to these principles, though, was never dogmatic; as many writers have noted, he was not averse to limited state intervention in the economy for relief of the needy, particularly the victims of the process by which industrial society was emerging.[76] However, this was a concession to political exigency, and was quite compatible with his basic contention that the inequality of fortune characterizing commercial societies—that is, the end product of unrestrained acquisitiveness—was natural and therefore just.

Tocqueville realized that equality of conditions would not mean equality of fortune: democracy would only succeed in replacing the arbitrary, conventional distribution of wealth prevailing in aristocratic ages with a more natural system.

The legislature [in a democracy], it is true, no longer grants privileges, but nature grants them. As natural inequality is very great, fortunes become unequal as soon as every man exerts all his faculties to get rich. . . . Natural inequality will soon make way for itself, and wealth will spontaneously pass into the hands of the most capable. Free and democratic communities, then,

---

[v] Tocqueville, *Democracy*, II, 168ff, 222–23; letter to Lord Radnor, Nov. 5, 1843, *Memoir*, II, 39. See also Salomon, "Tocqueville, 1959," p. 451: "Likewise he shared the faith of the liberals in classical economics, repeatedly contending that the laws of economics are eternal, not transitory, and that the radical workers should be indoctrinated with the true teachings of classical economics."

will always contain a multitude of people enjoying opulence or a competency.[77]

Mill wisely observed that Tocqueville assumed the democratic revolution would continue "until all artificial inequalities shall have disappeared from among mankind; those inequalities only remaining which are the natural and inevitable effects of the protection of property."[78] Tocqueville reaffirms his basic position on the inequalities of fortune in describing the June Days of 1848 in his *Recollections*. The working-class insurrectionists, he maintains, had been told not only that their poverty was the result of "unlawful oppression," but also that "the wealth of the rich was in some way the produce of a theft" from the workers. They had also been assured that inequality of fortune was "as opposed to morality and the welfare of society as it was to nature." Unfortunately, he states, "many had believed this obscure and erroneous notion of right."[w]

On the one hand, then, Tocqueville states that the unrestrained pursuit of material well-being leads to mediocrity, atomism, and the decline if not the eventual disappearance of civic virtue. On the other, he admits that the unrestrained pursuit of material well-being arises inevitably under democratic conditions; that the principles by which it is justified are incontestably true; and that the inequality of fortune in which it results is both natural and just. Moreover, he acknowledges both the power of the spirit of acquisitiveness and its social utility. A paradox indeed.

But Tocqueville is rarely content to deal with abstractions alone, and his analysis of the implementation of a principle is often more enlightening than his exposition of

---

[w] Tocqueville, *Recollections*, pp. 150-51. Tocqueville, like Locke, justifies the unequal distribution of wealth not only by its natural origin, but also by its contribution to the well-being of society as a whole. The poor suffer, he maintains, when they tamper with the fortunes of the rich. Cf. *Democracy*, I, 222.

the principle itself. Let us look, then, at his opinions on the acquisitiveness that seems to pervade America.

In Europe we are wont to look upon a restless disposition, an unbounded desire of riches, and an excessive love of independence as propensities very dangerous to society. Yet these are the very elements that ensure a long and peaceful future to the republics of America. Without these unquiet passions the population would collect in certain spots and would soon experience wants like those of the Old World, which it is difficult to satisfy; for such is the present good fortune of the New World that the vices of its inhabitants are scarcely less favorable to society than their virtues. These circumstances exercise a great influence on the estimation in which human actions are held in the two hemispheres. What we should call cupidity, the Americans frequently term a laudable industry; and they blame as faint-heartedness what we consider to be the virtue of moderate desires.[79]

The passage calls to mind again Mandeville's doctrine of "private vices, public virtues," vices here serving the socially useful function of developing an untouched continent. But the passage raises several questions. It is not clear, for example, if Tocqueville agrees with those who consider cupidity a vice. He is also very vague about the alleged necessity that transforms vices into virtues. Why did the Americans *have* to fill the continent? Why did they have to adapt it to commerce and industry? Why could not the Americans, like their neighbors to the North, have restrained their acquisitive passions and kept their nation at a modest size? There is no question that Tocqueville discounts the importance of the Americans' physical environment in accounting for their acquisitive drives.[80] The passion for wealth did not arise because of the opportunities for gain; it will not disappear if those opportunities diminish. As we have seen, the desire for well-being inevitably accompanies equality of conditions, quite independently of climatic or geographic fac-

tors. But accepting acquisitiveness as a "given" of democratic times does not relieve one of the obligation to evalu-
ate it.

Tocqueville's evaluation, I believe, may be seen in his
attitude toward the Americans' conquest of their continent.
Generally, he approves, as his readiness to accept the dis-
placement of the Indians suggests. The reason for his ap-
proving attitude is apparently a preference for large states
—a preference that, as is Tocqueville's wont, is never made
explicit. About the most he will acknowledge is that "the
existence of great nations is unavoidable," and that this being the case, it is better to be among the powerful than the
weak.[81] Even this statement is preceded by a classical defense of the small state as the natural home of freedom.
For one so passionately devoted to freedom, this alone
might be expected to be decisive. However, Tocqueville's
argument then takes an unusual and surprising turn. "In
small states . . . the powers of every individual being generally limited, his desires are proportionately small. Mediocrity of fortune makes the various conditions of life nearly
equal, and the manners of the inhabitants are orderly and
simple." Such a people may be free and happy, but they
cannot be great.

For the very reason that the desire for power is more intense in
[large] communities than among ordinary men, the love of
glory is also more developed in the hearts of certain citizens [of
these large communities], who regard the applause of a great
people as a reward worthy of their exertions and an elevating
encouragement to men. If we would learn why great nations
contribute more powerfully to the increase of knowledge and
the advance of civilization than small states, we shall discover
an adequate cause in the more rapid and energetic circulation of
ideas in those great cities which are the intellectual centers where
all the rays of human genius are reflected and combined. To
this it may be added that most important discoveries demand a

use of national power which the government of a small state is unable to make: in great nations the government has more enlarged ideas, and is more completely disengaged from the routine of precedent and the selfishness of local feeling; its designs are conceived with more talent and executed with more boldness.[x]

Tocqueville does not hesitate to declare that in America, the image of democracy itself, there is only one "energetic passion" that can support the drive to become a great nation—the love of wealth.[82] Curiously enough, he believes that the pursuit of wealth may even mitigate democracy's neglect of the arts and sciences, for affluence will give at least some citizens the leisure and ability to devote themselves to these pursuits. That they will also have the inclination to do so he gratuitously assumes: "In those pleasures they will indulge, for if it is true that the human mind leans on one side to the limited, the material, and the useful, it naturally rises on the other to the infinite, the spiritual, and the beautiful. Physical wants confine it to the earth, but when they no longer hold it down, it will rise of itself."[83] His expectations are not confined to the affluent few: with the social barriers to wealth overturned, each citizen will perceive how inequality of fortune results from the natural diversity of talent; and, so enlightened, will pursue all forms of knowledge in order to maximize his talents and thereby increase his fortune. In the process, the cultural level of society as a whole will be raised.

The spirit of commerce, then, both mitigates against the leveling effects of democracy and provides a spur to gran-

[x] Tocqueville, *Democracy*, I, 165, 167–68. Tocqueville's preference for large states over small ones may be interpreted as indicating that he does not regard freedom as unqualifiedly the highest good. He writes, "La liberté [est] la condition nécessaire sans laquelle il n'y a jamais eu de nation véritablement grande et virile." (Liberty is the precondition without which there has never been a truly great and vigorous nation.) Tocqueville to Beaumont, Feb. 27, 1858, in *Oeuvres Complètes* (Beaumont), VII, 488.

deur. Montesquieu had pointed out that this spirit was entirely consistent with social stability and a kind of quiet morality:

True it is that when a democracy is founded on commerce, private people may acquire vast riches without a corruption of morals. This is because the spirit of commerce is naturally attended with that of frugality, economy, moderation, labor, prudence, tranquillity, order, and rule. So long as this spirit subsists, the riches it produces have no bad effect. The mischief is when excessive wealth destroys the spirit of commerce; then it is that the inconveniences of inequality begin to be felt.[y]

Tocqueville also acknowledges that the commercial spirit promotes social stability:

Commerce is naturally adverse to all the violent passions: it loves to temporize, takes delight in compromise, and studiously avoids irritation. It is patient, insinuating, flexible, and never has recourse to extreme measures until obliged by the most absolute necessity. Commerce renders men independent of one another, gives them a lofty notion of their personal importance, leads them to seek to conduct their own affairs, and teaches how to conduct them well; it therefore prepares men for freedom, but preserves them from revolutions.[84]

Tocqueville believed that the spirit of commerce would produce a social state in which most men owned some property, thus ending the contrast between the few rich and the many poor that he considered the main source of social instability. "Either the poor have attempted to plunder the rich, or the rich to enslave the poor. If, then, a state of society can ever be founded in which every man shall have something to keep and little to take from others, much will have been done for the peace of the world."[85] A free, dem-

[y] Montesquieu, p. 46. The last sentence of this quotation brings to mind the forces that Tocqueville feared would give rise to a new aristocracy.

ocratic, and commercial community would be such a state.

It is important to emphasize that the "quiet" character of the commercial spirit refers to social stability, not opposition to energy and activity. It is not the sort of spirit that sets men apart from or against one another.[z] However, it does generate zeal; and one is not likely to find a society that it dominates to be static or to have a high regard for the contemplative life. Like many political theorists of the modern age, Tocqueville was biased in favor of societal activity, almost apart from any end it was to serve; in part, of course, this was a corollary of his devotion to freedom. In 1829, he wrote that the only virtue he valued in man was energy; nearly thirty years later, he still maintained that the "world belongs to the energetic."[aa] In the *Democracy*, he noted that "Democracy does not give the people the most skillful government, but it produces what the ablest governments are frequently unable to create: namely, an all-pervading and restless activity, a superabundant force, and an energy which is inseparable from it and which may, however unfavorable circumstances may be, produce wonders. These are the true advantages of democracy."[86]

In his *Journey to England*, Tocqueville observed the similarity between the requirements of a free life and those of a life of commerce:

To be free one must have the capacity to plan and persevere in a difficult undertaking, and be accustomed to act on one's own; to live in freedom one must grow used to a life full of agitation, change and danger; to keep alert the whole time with a restless eye on everything around: that is the price of freedom. All those qualities are equally needed for success in commerce. . . .[87]

---

[z] See Strauss, pp. 187–88. Tocqueville does encourage a form of pride not inconsistent with social harmony—see pp. 135–36 below.

[aa] Tocqueville to Beaumont, Oct. 29, 1829, *Memoir*, I, 414; to Alexis Stoffels, Dec. 12, 1856, *Memoir*, II, 408. Cf. *Democracy*, II, 150: "Certainly it is not to be inferred that nations ought to despise public tranquillity; but that state ought not to content them."

This passage is accompanied by a marginal note: "Why then should one say that freedom is the mother of trade, and not trade the father of freedom?" Montesquieu had argued that the spirit of trade naturally gave rise to the spirit of liberty; Tocqueville, as Drescher has pointed out, insisted on reversing the causal relationship.[88] Tocqueville presents his views very tentatively. If he had the time, he tells us, he could explain why liberty gives birth to trade. He notes that although some peoples have been free without being either manufacturers or traders, he can find no examples of commercial peoples who were not free. Logically, he ought to have concluded that freedom alone cannot generate the spirit of commerce; but he does not. He is left with the "hidden relationship" between liberty and trade that is the subject of his query. He asserts that the extensive opportunities for commerce that were available to the English, for example (outlets to the sea, access to natural resources, and the like), were not responsible for the commercial spirit that did arise in England. The real reason for its emergence lay in "the turn given to the human spirit in England by political life." He concludes:

Do you want to test whether a people is given to industry and commerce? Do not sound its ports, or examine the wood from its forests or the produce of its soil. The spirit of trade will get all these things, and without it, they are useless. Examine whether this people's laws give men the courage to seek prosperity, freedom to follow it up, the sense and habits to find it, and the assurance of reaping the benefit.[89]

Yet, far from demonstrating that freedom generates a taste for commerce, Tocqueville shows instead how such laws would only reflect a people's previous commitment to commercial goals and aspirations. If a people assumed the legitimacy and desirability of commercial activity, their political life might naturally be expected to provide a framework for commerce, and even to attempt to cultivate a taste for it. But the assumption itself would not make sense from Tocqueville's point of view unless it could be shown that a commercial order is instrumental in achieving not only material wealth, but also non-economic goods like political stability and individual freedom. He himself did not present an analysis of the non-economic benefits of a commercial order, but precisely such an argument was common to the thought of the early modern economic philosophers—Locke, Montesquieu, and Adam Smith, for example. It must have been the acceptance of at least the principle of this argument that permitted Tocqueville to appeal to the spirit of commerce in attempting to resolve the problem of democracy.[90]

If the idea that a commercial order can achieve non-economic goods is granted, there is more than a little justification for proposing a simple substitution in the Puritans' formula for a good society: to replace, in their amalgam of "the spirit of liberty and the spirit of religion," the spirit of religion with that of commerce. It is surprising how much commerce and religion have in common. Like religious fervor, the spirit of commerce prompts men to acts of courage and privation. Men in democratic ages are at least as ready to risk their lives in the pursuit of well-being as in that of salvation: the lure of quick and easy gain overcomes even the fear of violent death. Commerce cannot thrive without a sense of foresight, and may thus supply the concern with the future that religion typically imparts to a society. Religion, at least every modern religion, cuts across national boundaries. So does commerce, for "cheapness is the sovereign law of commerce," and "sovereign will and national prejudices cannot long resist the influence of cheapness." Money and the profit motive are also universal. It is even conceivable that commerce, in coming to dominate men's concern, might serve as the unifying principle of democratic society; that it might become the cement of society, as religion was before it. Religion, of course, had always been the mainstay of public morality, but Tocqueville repeatedly emphasizes that a commercial society must by its very nature be moral and orderly. Both religion and commerce prepare men for freedom—the one by restraining men from abusing it, the other by encouraging the development of prudence and temperance. Finally, either religion or commerce, each in its own way, may foster the noble urge to explore the higher reaches of human experience.[91]

But it would be erroneous to suppose that Tocqueville ever envisaged a commercial, democratic society that did not need religion. The problem of democracy is so acute that statesmen would be foolish to forsake any remedy; and in Tocqueville's thought commerce and religion complement, reinforce, and sometimes even counterbalance each other's tendencies. Religion inhibits the vulgarization of society by commerce; commerce reawakens men to a just appreciation of the human sphere.

Considered from the point of view of the interests of this world, commerce and religion do differ in one important respect: the spirit of commerce makes men independent and gives them a "lofty notion of their own importance"; the spirit of religion makes men realize their dependence on each other and on a social order greater than any one of them. The one encourages pride, the other humility. Greatness of soul or deed may be the product of either spirit, depending on which best fits the needs and the temperament of a particular epoch. The paramount need in democratic ages is, paradoxically, pride. Individualism, by centering a man's thoughts entirely on his own desires, gives rise to the problem of democracy. What begins with a species of pride threatens, because of the feeling of impotence that equality of conditions generates, to transform itself into the most abject humility. And Tocqueville fears much more from the mediocrity of men's passions than he does from the unleashing of their ambitions:

Moralists are constantly complaining that the ruling vice of the present time is pride. This is true in one sense, for indeed everyone thinks that he is better than his neighbor or refuses to obey his superior; but it is extremely false in another, for the same man who cannot endure subordination or equality has so contemptible an opinion of himself that he thinks he is born only to indulge in vulgar pleasures. He willingly takes up with low desires without daring to embark on lofty enterprises, of which he scarcely dreams. Thus, far from thinking that humility ought to be preached to our contemporaries, I would have endeavors made to give them a more enlarged idea of themselves and of their kind. Humility is unwholesome to them; what they most want is, in my opinion, pride. I would willingly exchange several of our small virtues for this one vice.[bb]

Tocqueville preserves in his writings the tradition of referring to self-centered attitudes or habits as "vices," but it should be clear that the term is mostly free of overtones of moral depravity. With the unrestrained acquisitive instinct in mind, he notes: "Carefully considering the greatness which the English people has now attained, I see many virtues among the causes of this greatness, but wonder if vices have not done even more."[92] If we recall that Tocqueville's resolution of the problem of democracy is based on self-in-

---

[bb] Tocqueville, *Democracy*, II, 261–62. Tocqueville considers the stultifying effect of mediocrity of ambition so great that even war may sometimes be necessary to overcome it. "I do not wish to speak ill of war; war almost always enlarges the mind of a people and raises their character. In some cases it is the only check to the excessive growth of certain propensities that naturally spring out of equality of conditions, and it must be considered as a necessary corrective to certain inveterate diseases to which democratic communities are liable." (*Ibid.*, p. 283.) See also Richter, pp. 362–98, especially p. 385: "[Tocqueville's] advocacy of imperialism was based on what he considered moral grounds: the European nations could escape from the selfishness of individualism only by undertaking great tasks."

terest rightly understood, the nature of this metamorphosis of vice into virtue becomes clear. To resolve the problem of democracy on the level of democracy one must utilize passions or forces that are compatible with or complement those unleashed by democracy. Whether these forces are virtues or vices in the traditional sense is immaterial: their efficacy in the task at hand is the sole criterion. The spirit of commerce aptly fills the bill of particulars; more than any other force, the unremitting drive for gain conforms to the doctrine of self-interest rightly understood.

At the outset of his inquiry into the nature of democracy and the problems to which it gives rise, Tocqueville makes this plea:

The first of the duties that are at this time imposed upon those who direct our affairs is to educate democracy; to reawaken, if possible, its religious beliefs; to purify its morals; to mold its actions; to substitute a knowledge of statecraft for its inexperience, and an awareness of its true interests for its blind instincts; to adapt its government to time and place, and to modify it according to men and to conditions. A new science of politics is needed for a new world.[93]

The preceding sections of this chapter have dealt with Tocqueville's program for educating democracy: the means he proposed for reawakening a concern for the common good, for rekindling faith, for arousing and implementing self-interest. On the whole, despite its novel elements, Tocqueville's program probably would not have struck even a classical political philosopher as unique; so it is strange that he felt compelled to call for a new science of politics. After all, new facts are not necessarily beyond the purview of traditional science. Nevertheless, Tocqueville claims that the traditional view of social and political phenomena as products of laws and institutions is defective. It is necessary, he argues, to reverse the relationship, to consider laws and institutions themselves as emanating from the fundamental cause of social and political phenomena—social condition. Political institutions and activities are but one facet of society itself; they never fail, in the end, "to become the image and expression of civil society."[94] Thinking of political entities in terms of social condition does not make the concept of political life meaningless, but it considerably diminishes the importance of political life as a social force. To Tocqueville, any analysis of democratic politics must begin, more or less, with an acceptance of equality of conditions and an assessment of the dual propensities—toward freedom, or toward slavery—inherent in it.

Tocqueville's claim for social condition as the first cause of social and political phenomena thus apparently justifies his call for a new science of politics. Yet the status of social condition as the fundamental cause in his work is ultimately ambiguous, and the distance separating his approach to politics from, say, the classical political philosophers' is far less than he would have us believe.

Albert Salomon describes Tocqueville as one of the first political philosophers to exhibit a "sociological consciousness," which Salomon defines as "the understanding of the dependence of human existence and its social forms upon social conditions, and the knowledge of the functioning of social institutions and of the rules of social activity."[95] If this dependence refers to social condition as the origin of and explanation for ideas, customs, and political institutions, it must be acknowledged that Tocqueville develops no consistent thesis along these lines. Even his contention on the first page of the *Democracy* that equality of conditions is "the fundamental fact from which all others seem to be derived" is not an unqualified assertion. There is additional evidence. For example, in his chapter on the "Philosophic Method of the Americans," Tocqueville only says that this method, which he traces to Descartes, "was discovered at a time when men were beginning to equalize and assimilate their conditions."[96] He does not pretend to show how a philosophic method arose from a given social condition; only that the gradual development of a democratic social condition facilitated the rediscovery of the method. One may well ask whether it was not the adoption of the doctrines of Descartes and the generalizations drawn from them that was responsible for the widespread equalizing of conditions, rather than the contrary. There is even a suggestion of the former interpretation in the *Democracy*:

The philosophical method of the eighteenth century, then, is not only French, but democratic; and this explains why it was so readily admitted throughout Europe, *where it has contributed so powerfully to change the face of society*. It is not because the French have changed their former opinions and altered their former manners that they have convulsed the world, but because they were the first to generalize and bring to light a philosophical method by the aid of which it became easy to attack all that was old and to open a path to all that was new.[97]

There is further evidence in the *Democracy* to show that Tocqueville does not consider social condition as something merely given, and to indicate its true role in his concept of society. We have only to recall his most important statement on the subject:

Social condition is commonly the result of circumstances [*d'un fait*], sometimes of laws, oftener still of these two causes united; but *when once established*, it may justly be considered as itself the source of *almost* all the laws, the usages [*coutumes*], and the ideas which regulate the conduct of nations.[cc]

[cc] Tocqueville, *Democracy*, I, 48, italics mine. For another indication of social condition's origin and role, see *Journey to America*, p. 161: "If nature has not given each people an indelible national character one must at least admit that physical or political causes have made a people's spirit adopt habits which are very difficult to eradicate, even though [that spirit] is no longer subject to the influence of any of those causes."

In another passage, he notes, "A law may modify the social condition [*l'état social*], which seems to be most fixed and determinate; and with the social condition everything must change."[98]

Taken together, these statements prove that social condition is not the prime mover of society in Tocqueville's thought. But if it is not, what is? Interestingly enough, a passage in the *Old Régime* that seems to support the primary role of social condition provides a clue to quite a different first cause:

It was not by mere chance that our eighteenth-century philosophers as a body enounced theories so strongly opposed to those that were still regarded as basic to the social order; they could hardly be expected to do otherwise when they contemplated the world around them. The sight of so many absurd or ridiculous privileges, whose effects were increasingly felt on every hand though their causes were less and less understood, urged or rather forced all of them simultaneously toward the idea of the natural equality of conditions. When they saw so many ridiculous, irregular institutions, survivals of an earlier age . . . it was natural enough that thinkers of the day should come to loathe everything that savored of the past and should desire to remold society on entirely new lines, traced by each thinker in the sole light of reason.[99]

It should be evident that men could not consider a condition of inequality as "absurd or ridiculous" without some prior idea of a condition that was not absurd or ridiculous, and some prior conclusion that such a condition would be preferable to one of inequality. What else but the idea that a better condition might be possible could dissatisfy men with their present lot, and make them desire to remold society? One can only conclude that ideas and not social conditions are primary in Tocqueville's thought, despite his emphasis on the latter.

The decisive role of ideas in Tocqueville's conception of politics is further concealed by the influence of an aspect of social life that is considered sometimes as an integral part of social condition, and sometimes as an independent factor itself. This is the influence of mores (*moeurs*). Tocqueville applies the term principally to "the various notions and opinions current among men, and to the mass of those ideas which constitute their character of mind."[100] The term thus conveys everything that "custom" does and more. In recognizing the important political role of mores, Tocqueville again follows the lead of both Montesquieu and Rousseau. Rousseau had suggested that "with mores the great legislator concerns himself in secret, though he seems to confine himself to particular regulations; for these are only the arc of the arch, while mores, slower to arise, form in the end its immovable keystone."[101] In the *Democracy*, while discussing the maintenance of democratic institutions in America, Tocqueville agrees with Rousseau:

The effect which the geographical position of a country may have upon the duration of democratic institutions is exaggerated in Europe. Too much importance is attributed to legislation, too little to mores. These three great causes serve, no doubt, to regulate and direct American democracy, but if they were to be classed in their proper order, I should say that physical circumstances are less efficient than the laws, and the laws less so than the mores of the people. I am convinced that the most advantageous situation and the best possible laws cannot maintain a constitution in spite of the mores of a country; while the latter may turn to some advantage the most unfavorable positions and the worst laws. The importance of mores is a common truth to which study and experience incessantly direct our attention. It may be regarded as a central point in the range of observation, and the common termination of all my inquiries. So seriously do I insist upon this head that, if I have hitherto failed in making the reader feel the important influence of the practical experience, the habits, the opinions, in short of the mores of the Americans upon the maintenance of their institutions, I have failed in the principal object of my work.[dd]

If mores and social condition exercise so compelling an influence, it may appear that the effectiveness of legislators is limited:

When, after many efforts, a legislator succeeds in exercising an indirect influence upon the destiny of nations, his genius is lauded by mankind, while, in point of fact, the geographical position of the country, which he is unable to change, a social condition which arose without his cooperation, mores and opinions which he cannot trace to their source, and an origin with which he is unacquainted exercise so irresistible an influence over the courses of society that he is himself borne away by the current after an ineffectual resistance. Like the navigator, he may direct the vessel which bears him, but he can neither change its structure, nor raise the winds, nor lull the waters that swell beneath him.[102]

But the simile of the navigator is misleading, for Tocqueville believes that the legislator does have the power to alter both the form and the material makeup of his vessel. The legislator does not have to take men as they are, or even as they are shaped by a condition of equality; rather, he is given the task of fundamentally changing men—from self-interested individuals to citizens. If mores or social condition were impervious to other forces, if they were in fact the unmoved movers of all else, Tocqueville's recourse to education, to ideology, and to institutional devices would be pointless. But mores and social condition only *seem* to

---

[dd] Tocqueville, *Democracy*, I, 334, translation amended. But mores are no more a first cause than social condition: in speaking of a worker's decreasing freedom of social movement in a society strictly organized on the principles of division of labor, Tocqueville notes that "a theory of manufactures more powerful than mores and laws binds him to a craft." (*Democracy*, II, 169, translation amended.)

have an independent existence: they can be and are affected by ideas. Once established, their influence can be turned to the legislator's advantage. It is not too much to suggest that Tocqueville, like Rousseau, thought that the legislator would concern himself with mores "in secret." His basic belief in the possibility of thus changing society is indicated in the *Democracy:* "The democratic revolution has taken place in the body of society without the concomitant change in the laws, ideas, customs, and mores [*les habitudes et les moeurs*] which was necessary to render such a revolution beneficial."[103] And further on, "The Americans have shown that it would be wrong to despair of regulating democracy by the aid of mores and laws."[104]

That Tocqueville's approach to the study of politics is classical in conception, his apparent emphasis on social condition notwithstanding, is made clear in an address he delivered to the Académie des Sciences Morales et Politiques in 1853. The role he assigns to political science is perhaps even more architectonic than the claims made on its behalf by Aristotle:

What the political sciences achieved [in the Revolution of 1789] with such irresistible force and brilliance they achieve everywhere and always, though more secretly and more slowly. Among all civilized peoples the political sciences give birth or at least form to those general concepts whence emerge the facts with which politicians have to deal, and the laws of which they believe themselves the inventors. [These general concepts] form a kind of atmosphere surrounding each society in which both rulers and governed have to draw intellectual breath, and whence—often without realizing it—both groups derive the principles of action. Only among barbarians does the practical side of politics exist alone.[105]

In the same address he asserts that the only constant in political matters is not any particular social condition, but the

nature of man himself. The "scientific" side of politics, he
tells us, is "founded in the very nature of man . . . his interests; his faculties; the needs revealed by philosophy and
history; the instincts which change their objects with the
times, but never change their nature, and are as immortal
as the race itself. It is this aspect [of political science] . . .
that teaches us what laws are most appropriate for the general and permanent condition of mankind."[106] To Tocqueville, the effectiveness of laws depends on the extent to
which they utilize the many forces that affect men politically; the effectiveness of political scientists depends on the
extent to which they help legislators to achieve an understanding of these forces. In his resolution of the problem of
democracy he aspires, like his classical predecessors, to be
the teacher of legislators.

IV

The Problem of Democracy Revisited

THE LIVES of some men are marked by an astonishing unity of purpose. Tocqueville's mission matured early; it is nowhere better described than in his well-known letter to Eugène Stoffels, written just before his twenty-seventh birthday:

What has always struck me most in my country . . . has been to see ranged on one side the men who value morality, religion, and order, and on the other those who love liberty and legal equality. To me this is as extraordinary as it is deplorable; for I am convinced that all the things which we thus separate are indissolubly united in the eyes of God. They are all *sacred*, if I may use the expression; man can be great and happy only when they are combined. From the time that I found this out I believed that one of the greatest achievements in our time would be to prove it, to show that all these advantages are not merely compatible but necessarily connected. Such is the outline of my idea. . . .

I have always loved liberty instinctively, and the more I reflect, the more convinced am I that neither political nor moral greatness can long subsist without it. At the same time, I hope to show so much respect for justice, such sincere love of order and law, such a deliberate attachment to morality and religion, that I cannot but believe that I shall be discovered to be a liberal of a new kind; not to be confounded with our ordinary modern democrats.[1]

Such was the outline of his life's work; such were the aspirations on whose commingled achievement depended any final resolution of the problem of democracy.

Tocqueville sees men as politically equal by nature, and acknowledges this political equality as the necessary basis of justice. The just commonwealth is thus inescapably democratic. But justice is not enough, for his investigations, both theoretical and empirical, also reveal to him the deleterious character of the passions unleashed by the drive for equality. Men must be more than equal; they must be free. But there is no reason to believe that unrestrained freedom for everyone will automatically be compatible with a healthy social order. For all his trust in one or another form of "invisible hand," Tocqueville refuses to go this far. Freedom has to be joined not only to equality, but also to morality, religion, and order. As equality is the precondition of justice, morality and order are the preconditions of greatness. Resolving the problem of democracy entails showing that none of these components *can* be sacrificed and, moreover, that none *need* be sacrificed, since together they constitute a harmonious unity.

At the end of Chapter II, I suggested that Tocqueville's ultimate purpose was to work out a political arrangement in which both justice and human excellence would flourish. Utopian as this goal may seem, it is scarcely as extreme as the one Leroy attributed to Tocqueville: "What [Tocqueville] hopes for is a State in which there will be only wise men. . . . Who has not hoped in a moment of optimism for a State equilibrated by the good will of equal and free men! But who has not quickly reprimanded himself for abandoning himself to this too facile phantasm! . . . I fear that [Tocqueville] remained right up to the end of his life dominated by this dream."[2] As we have seen, Tocqueville had no such illusions. Not all would be wise; but the foolish must not reduce everyone to their own level under the banner of equality. Not all would be excellent, or virtuous; but some approximation to excellence and virtue must become the aspiration of most men. Not all would wish to devote themselves to public affairs; but some encouragement must be given to public-spiritedness lest men remain so completely absorbed in private pursuits that they lose forever the capacity for self-enlargement that comes with collective efforts.

Nevertheless, Tocqueville's effort to demonstrate the necessary and indissoluble unity of the components of a just and viable democratic society did not succeed. The evidence is unmistakable. First, his reliance on salutary myths (such as the inevitability thesis) suggests a strategy of persuasion rather than of demonstration; though such myths may be useful, self-deception is questionable in a system purportedly based on self-enlightenment. Second, his concessions to the spirit of democracy seem to be compromises with the spirit of excellence. The doctrine of self-interest rightly understood, for example, is advocated not as the best moral teaching, but as the most appropriate for the time. And the doctrine itself cannot support the burden it is made to assume. Third, far from effecting a synthesis of religion and liberty, Tocqueville manages only to reconcile spiritualistic myths with a drive for freedom so distorted by materialistic overtones that it is incompatible with freedom's usual meaning. Fourth, Tocqueville never succeeds in establishing patriotism and public-spiritedness on a firm footing. In the end, it becomes clear that if he succeeded at all, he succeeded in combining not genuine liberty, genuine morality or religion, and genuine patriotism; but a species of liberty, a species of morality or religion, and a species of patriotism—each of which contrasts strikingly with its real counterpart.

Tocqueville himself came to realize this—as we can see, for example, by examining how his understanding of freedom changed and deepened over the years. In his early writings, he seeks to attach liberty to equality by the doctrine of self-interest: men are to be taught that liberty is essential to their well-being. In the *Democracy* he observes that men in democratic times need freedom to procure the goods they long for. The Americans are a good example:

> [They] alternately display so strong and so similar a passion for their own welfare [*bien-être*] and for their freedom that it may be supposed that these passions are united and mingled in some part of their character. And indeed, the Americans believe their freedom to be the best instrument and surest safeguard of their welfare; they are attached to the one by the other.[3]

In short, freedom in his early work is regarded primarily as an instrument of private interest. In his later writings, however, particularly in the *Old Régime* and the notes for its sequel, Tocqueville takes a different view. He distinguishes between a genuine love of freedom and one based on private interest:

> *I do not think any longer* that a genuine love of freedom is ever quickened by the prospect of material rewards; indeed that prospect is often dubious . . . True, in the long run freedom always brings to those who know how to retain it comfort and well-being, and often great prosperity. Nevertheless, for the moment it sometimes tells against amenities of this nature, and there are times, indeed, when despotism can best ensure a brief enjoyment of them. In fact, those who prize freedom only for the material benefits it offers have never kept it long.[4]

The genuine love of freedom has its own attraction, "quite apart from any material advantage."[5] Those who have never felt it can scarcely be made to comprehend its nature. A devotion to freedom arising from calculation (*d'une idée raisonnée*) may be nurtured; Tocqueville attempts to nurture it in the *Democracy*. But the genuine love of freedom (*d'un sentiment instinctif*), the love of freedom for its own sake, is unteachable:

Where will people get their real taste for liberty if they do not know it or if they have lost it? Who will teach them these noble pleasures? Who can make them love liberty if that love has not been originally planted in their hearts? Who will even pretend to make them understand those pleasures of liberty which men can no longer even imagine once they have lost their habitual experience? . . . Material interest will never be sufficiently permanent and tangible to maintain the love of liberty in the hearts of men unless their taste for it exists.[6]

The real taste for freedom is "born out of the mysterious sources of all great human passions."[7] It does not and cannot arise from self-interest, and, unlike the taste for freedom so generated, it will not wane if material advantages are lost.

Just as his more mature views reflect a preference for the kind of freedom that is impervious to the promptings of self-interest, so, too, his more considered thoughts on patriotism show the importance of his attempt to give public-spiritedness a foundation that would make it unshakable by mere utilitarian considerations.[8] Without such a foundation, he could not resolve the problem of democracy as he saw it, for a lasting sense of patriotism, one resistant to the pressures of democratic forces, was central to his endeavor. As Doris Goldstein has noted, "That [civic virtue] must exist, that it must be made to exist, through whatever ideological or institutional devices available, is both the core of Tocqueville's concept of citizenship and one of the important motifs of his political philosophy. Without civic virtue the future of modern democracies would be bleak, while its existence would open the way to a good society."[9] In fact, however, his views on patriotism are ambiguous or inconsistent, reflecting uncertainties in his own thought that reflect, in turn, the opposing tendencies of the democratic predicament.

In a note prepared for the sequel to the *Old Régime*,

Tocqueville makes his strongest plea for the consideration of patriotism as a virtue rooted in the nature of man:

From a general, higher viewpoint patriotism, despite its great impulses and deeds, would seem a false and narrow passion. The great efforts suggested by patriotism are in reality due to humanity, and not to those small fragments of the human race within particular limits called peoples or nations. It would seem, at first sight, that those Christian moralists especially who are inclined to care more for humanity than for their fatherland are right. Yet this is but a detour, at the end of which we will find that they are wrong.

Man has been created by God (I do not know why) in such a way that the larger the object of his love the less directly attached he is to it. His heart needs particular passions; he needs limited objects for his affections to keep these firm and enduring. There are but few who will burn with ardent love for the entire human species. For the most part, the sole means by which Providence (man taken as he is) lets each of us work for the general good of humanity is to divide this great object into many smaller parts, making each of these fragments a worthy object of love to those who compose it. If everyone fulfills his duties in that way (and within these limits such duties are not beyond anyone's natural capacities if properly directed by morals and reason), the general good of humanity would be produced by the many, despite the absence of more direct efforts except by a few. *I am convinced that the interests of the human race are better served by giving every man a particular fatherland than by trying to inflame his passions for the whole of humanity.*[10]

A world state in which all national boundaries were dissolved would thus be both unnatural and contrary to the general welfare of mankind.

In the context of this conception of patriotism, it is clear that Tocqueville's appeal to the clergy for aid in fostering civic virtue does not conflict with his conviction that separation of church and state is necessary:

I do not ask the clergy to make those whom it educates, or influences, conscientiously Republicans or Royalists. But I wish it to tell them more frequently that while Christians, they also belong to one of the great human societies which God has formed, apparently in order to show more clearly the ties by which individuals ought to be mutually attached—societies which are called nations, inhabiting a territory which they call their country. I wish the clergy to instil into their very souls [the idea] that everyone belongs much more to this collective Being than he does to himself; that towards this Being no one ought to be indifferent, much less, by treating such indifferences as a sort of languid virtue, to enervate one of our noblest instincts; that everyone is responsible for the fortunes of this collective Being; that everyone is bound to work out its prosperity, and to watch that it be not governed except by respectable, beneficent, and legitimate authorities.[a]

Since man's nature is such that he needs a limited center of his affections, patriotism—affection for one's country—is

---

[a] Tocqueville to Madame Swetchine, Oct. 20, 1856, in *Memoir*, II, 333–34; cf. Rousseau, pp. 113-14, 251-52. For an extended discussion of Tocqueville's appeal to the clergy, see Goldstein, "Tocqueville's Concept of Citizenship," pp. 48-53. Goldstein maintains that although Tocqueville agreed with Rousseau that "religion must make good citizens as well as good men," he did not share Rousseau's belief "that Christianity was inherently incapable of fulfilling this function because it diverts men from the duties of citizenship" (*ibid.*, p. 51). Tocqueville certainly did not share Rousseau's enthusiasm for a purely secular religion, but it is not at all evident that he ever resolved his doubts about Christianity's ability to fulfill religion's social function—the doubts he expressed to Gobineau, for example: "Christianity and consequently its morality went beyond all political powers and nationalities. Its grand achievement is to have formed a human community beyond national societies. The duties of men among themselves as well as in their capacity of *citizens*, the duties of citizens to their fatherland, in brief, the public virtues seem to me to have been inadequately defined and considerably neglected within the moral system of Christianity" (Sept. 5, 1843, in Tocqueville, *European Revolution*, p. 192).

natural; since the general welfare of humanity is best pro-
moted by encouraging patriotism, it must be recognized as
the foremost moral imperative. In fact, the note on patriotism just cited is headed "How Patriotism is Justified in the
Eyes of Reason and Appears to it not only a Great Virtue
but the First."

Tocqueville's celebration of the nation-state was not, of
course, the product of any kind of chauvinistic passion. He
thought patriotism was needed to counteract the forces in
modern society that were breaking down the bonds between
men, destroying national and cultural traditions, and generally producing a uniform mediocrity of mankind. From the
moment he conceived his lifework, Tocqueville had pon-
dered the effect these forces might have on men's chances
for greatness. In December 1831, he wrote in his notebook:

If ever the world comes to be completely civilized, the human
race will in appearance form only one people. Reason, like virtue,
does not bend at all in different climates, and does not vary with
temperaments and the nature of places. It is one, it is inflexible.
Everywhere it tends to the same end, and progresses by the same
roads. All the peoples, then, that take reason for the guide of their
actions must have great points of resemblance: to think, to believe, to feel the same things in a whole lot of circumstances. On
the other hand, when a people takes as its model a certain ideal
perfection peculiar to it, when it is concerned to do as its fathers
did and not to do the best possible, when it follows custom and
not reasoning, it stays completely itself; and time only adds to
the differences that separate it from its neighbors. Does not the
change that takes away from a people its originality and its physiognomy also take away part of its nationality and its individual
vigor? That is what seems to me to be in question.[b]

---

[b] Tocqueville, *Journey to America*, p. 163; cf. *Democracy*, II, 240–41: "All
the nations which take not any particular man, but Man himself as the object
of their researches and their imitations are tending in the end to a similar state
of society."

With scarcely any reservation, Tocqueville answers his question affirmatively. Everything that tends to emphasize the basic similarity of the peoples of mankind diminishes the opportunities for excellence that appear to be bound up with national and cultural individuality. The principle of equality collaborates with the forces of reason and civilization in accelerating the trend toward uniformity by emphasizing each man's self to the exclusion of his responsibilities toward his country. In the passage just cited Tocqueville mentions two conflicting types of excellence, that achieved by following the dictates of pure reason (the "best possible") and that achieved by living up to the model of "ideal perfection" peculiar to a particular people or nation. Tocqueville acknowledges the claims of both kinds of excellence but lends his support to the one whose survival under democratic conditions is uncertain. He seeks, then, to revitalize the virtue of patriotism, one that has the effect of separating a particular group from the rest of mankind.

Tocqueville expected that a revivified patriotism would differ from traditional patriotism—it would be quieter, less heroic, less ardent, and more intimately tied to the personal interests of each citizen. Yet he knew, of course, that patriotism was a matter of passionate concern to his contemporaries: the call for liberty, equality, and fraternity still echoed. Tocqueville located the source of what to him were aberrant passions in certain appeals to allegedly universal principles:

The French Revolution's approach to the problems of man's existence here on earth was exactly similar to that of the religious revolutions as regards his afterlife. It viewed the "citizen" from an abstract angle, that is to say as an entity independent of any particular social order, just as religions view the individual without regard to nationality or the age he lives in. It did not aim merely at defining the rights of the French citizen, but sought also to determine the rights and duties of men in general toward each other and as members of a body politic. It was because the Revolution always harked back to universal, not particular, values, and to what was the most "natural" social system, that it had so wide an appeal and could be imitated in so many places simultaneously.[c]

Thus, despite his emphasis on the quietness of democratic patriotism, Tocqueville was well aware of the possibilities for explosive patriotism inherent in the appeal to universal values. Moreover, he provided the theoretical basis for comprehending how easy and even how necessary it is for these values to be linked with the interests of a particular nation or regime, so that the defense of these values becomes inseparable from the defense of the fatherland.

Perhaps democratic patriotism has been unquiet because modern man has managed to reconcile two very different impulses. One is abstract, appealing to men's universal aspirations; the other is concrete and localized, appealing to the immediate material interests of the citizens of a particular regime. Tocqueville saw both as natural and legitimate, and so does democratic man: he justifies his attachment to his homeland by associating it with what he believes is the only rationally defensible way of life. In short, democratic man subscribes to a national ideology that he believes to be based on universal truths. Patriotism in the modern world seems to take the form of participation in the struggle between competing national ideologies, though their "national" character is minimized because of the need to appeal to universal principles. Tocqueville's call for a democratic solution to the problem of democracy is a call for a solution

---

[c] Tocqueville, *Old Régime,* p. 12; cf. *European Revolution,* pp. 84–85: "Every Frenchman was convinced that not only was the government of France to be reformed, but that new principles of government were to be introduced into the world, applicable to all the nations of the earth and destined to remodel the entirety of human affairs; that in his hands lay not only the destiny of his own country but the fate of mankind."

that will satisfy democratic man's demands for material well-being as well as for universal principles. Although Tocqueville tended to think that the demand for well-being would predominate, and to regard quiet, calculating patriotism as the modern norm, he realized the strength of, and even made provision for, a democratic patriotism that could appeal to a universal principle—be it rights of men, history, Providence, equality, or some other.

He provides for this eventuality by implicitly encouraging the construction of *arbitrary* national ideologies to bind citizens together. These ideologies may justly be regarded as nationalistic myths analogous to the spiritualistic myths he also encourages. Indeed, Tocqueville's argument for the necessity of spiritualistic myths arises specifically in the context of a discussion of the need for a body of faith to unite *citizens*. The truth or falsity of national ideologies is as irrelevant to his purpose as was the content of religious dogma. The necessity for nationalistic myths arises from the fact that equality makes men conscious of their common humanity and may thus hinder the formation or promotion of nation-states that are erected on a claim for the superiority or at least the uniqueness of a portion of mankind. Some form of myth—or ideology, in the modern world—is needed to make men aware of their obligations to their fellow citizens, as distinguished from their obligations to their fellow men. But, as I pointed out above, Tocqueville identified the natural as that common to all men; and anything, be it moral code or national creed, that tends to separate men—to create differences between citizens of different regimes—is unnatural.[11] But patriotism or civic virtue is impossible without the erection of distinctions between regimes; if they do not arise from nature, they must be invented and fostered by art. We reach the paradoxical conclusion that patriotism rests not on nature but on convention.

Apart from the practical dangers inherent in stimulating

competitive national ideologies, Tocqueville is unable to resolve the tension between patriotism (which rejects the essential similarity of all men) and equality and reason (which affirm it). By Tocqueville's own reasoning, this conflict must end in the victory of equality and reason, the forces of justice and civilization. As nations come to share a common ideology, as men come to prize the bonds that unite them as men above the forces that separate them as citizens—in short, as natural values come to replace conventional ones—the "originality and physiognomy" of nations will fade away, and the kind of greatness that Tocqueville believes to arise from their uniqueness will no longer be possible.

The status of patriotism ultimately remains ambiguous in Tocqueville's political thought. His attempt to find a place within the democratic spirit for greatness and civic virtue can be considered as an attempt to substitute the conventional values of patriotism and civic virtue for the values suggested by reason and nature. The justification of patriotism as a *natural* virtue is, after all, addressed to the generality of men; he might well have reasoned otherwise if he were addressing, say, "the wise and the virtuous." That justification has a weakness, if not a flaw: it invokes the aid of some kind of invisible hand to transform the efforts of a people for its own good into efforts for the good of humanity as a whole. The process is not automatic; men must be persuaded that patriotism is a virtue, and this achievement cannot be guaranteed. Tocqueville's work presents the unusual paradox of an attempt to convince men of the supreme value of political virtue, accompanied by a depreciation of political or conventional values and an advocacy of natural ones. The opposition between devotion to one's own interests and devotion to those one shares with all men is not resolved in his writings. He shows that democracy is just, but until public and private interests can be reconciled without resort to myth, until the status of patriotism can be unequivocally affirmed, the question of whether democracy can also be great must remain open.

Self-interest rightly understood was the principal agency through which Tocqueville sought to resolve the problem of democracy. If he failed, finally, to achieve a genuine synthesis of justice and excellence, of nature and convention, of universality and uniqueness, the cause of his failure lay in the defects of that doctrine. The *Democracy*'s chapter on self-interest closes with this appeal:

I do not think that the system of self-interest as it is professed in America is in all its parts self-evident, but it contains a great number of truths so evident that men, if they are only educated, cannot fail to see them. Educate, then, at any rate, for the age of implicit self-sacrifice and instinctive virtues is already flitting far away from us, and the time is fast approaching when freedom, public peace, and social order itself will not be able to exist without education.[12]

But the sovereign masses have a limited intellectual capacity: "We may rest assured that the majority of mankind will always remain in one of these two states, will either believe they know not wherefore, or will not know what to believe. Few are those who can ever attain to that other state of rational and independent conviction which true knowledge can produce out of the midst of doubt."[13] Where there is no enlightenment, there can be no enlightened self-interest.

It can, of course, be argued that Tocqueville only adjusted his sights to the fundamental limitations of the democratic condition—that the doctrine of self-interest rightly understood, however imperfect, was the only doctrine capable of leading to some sort of greatness or excellence without violating the inviolable principle of equality. There is nothing inherently undemocratic in this doctrine—nothing inherently undemocratic, for example, in seeking to temper, moderate, delay, or enlighten the opinion of the sovereign majority through such devices as the separation of powers and indirect elections. Even Hofstadter's just criticism of the Founding Fathers is only partially applicable to Tocqueville. Hofstadter writes that the Founders "had no hope and they offered none for any ultimate organic change in the way men conduct themselves. The result was that while they thought self-interest the most dangerous and unbrookable quality of man, they necessarily underwrote it in trying to control it."[14] Tocqueville, by contrast, had higher hopes for self-interest: he hoped its enlightened application would bring about something approximating a fundamental change in man's nature. But it is precisely here that difficulties arise. On the one hand, it seems inherently unlikely that self-interest seen in terms of material well-being (the terms in which democratic men would see it) can lead to any genuine moral transformation. On the other hand, the attempt to view religion, for example, as a mere extension of the doctrine of self-interest leads inevitably to a restriction of democratic man's freedom to inquire and decide for himself. The myths to which such extensions give rise are not self-imposed, but are designed expressly to exempt from democratic inquiry certain matters best not inquired into. A man or a regime that believes in such myths, knowing not wherefore, is not autonomous and is not democratic. By resorting to myth, Tocqueville confessed his failure to resolve the problem of democracy on the level of democracy.

The prerequisite of democratic society is the education of men in the necessary restraints upon themselves, in preparation for higher and more noble pursuits. A healthy democracy, as Faguet remarked, must be more attentive to its interests than to its passions.[15] In particular, a healthy democracy requires that its citizens recognize their true interests; that they be educated to place these interests ahead of their passions, however persistent or deeply felt; that this education be accomplished on a reasonably permanent basis, so that democratic life is not a constant struggle between interest and passion; and finally, as Rousseau recognized, that the effect precede the cause, that men who are not yet citizens apply to themselves the restraints of citizens.[16] The problem of democracy has never been better stated than by Faguet: "In truth, the only remedies for the dangers of Democracy are that Democracy should moderate itself of its own accord, should put the brakes on itself, so to speak; and such brakes can only be bodies having more or less an aristocratic character; but Democracy will never permit such bodies within itself; so, as Montaigne said, here we are arguing round in a circle."[d]

If Tocqueville seems sometimes to make the optimistic claim that this vicious circle can be broken by one or another of his democratic expedients, or by the salutary operation of some "invisible hand," a closer reading will show that he had no such expectation. He never thought of democratic expedients except as temporary palliatives, and he knew that no permanent solution was possible without a fundamental change in the nature of men. The core of his teaching about democracy is hardly hopeful. Nature dissociates men, at least in their civil capacities; it encourages them to think wholly of themselves, and to regard their self-centered enterprise as the just sum of their energies and obligations. Only art or myth can turn their gaze outward, and this not

---

[d] Curiously, Faguet himself remained optimistic by suggesting (p. 108) that democracy "without wanting, simply by the functioning of its mechanism," does create an aristocratic body within its midst, namely a bureaucracy, that is conservative and able to moderate the passions of democracy. Apart from the question of whether bureaucracies are formed in this way, the adequacy of Faguet's solution depends on whether or not the bureaucracy takes on the characteristics of an alien force within democracy: if it does, and is seen as alien, it may not be tolerated; but if it is in fact not alien, it will not solve the problem of democracy.

with nature's blessing or concurrence, but in defiance of nature or behind its back. In political terms, what Leo Strauss reconstructs as Rousseau's teaching on the nature of a free society applies equally to Tocqueville's view of democracy: "Society must do everything possible to render the citizens oblivious of the very facts that political philosophy brings to the center of their attention as the foundations of society. Free society stands or falls by a specific obfuscation against which political philosophy necessarily revolts."[17]

Notes

Notes

Complete authors' names, titles, and publication data may be found in the Bibliography, pp. 173–77.

I

1. Leroy, p. 489.
2. *Ibid.*, p. 482.
3. Keeney, p. 62.
4. Schapiro, pp. 550–51.
5. Salomon, "Tocqueville, 1959," p. 465; see also Wyndham Lewis, pp. 557–75, and Gargan, "Reply to Wyndham Lewis," pp. 6–7.
6. Tocqueville, *Democracy*, II, 351. Unless otherwise indicated, all references to the *Democracy* are to the Vintage edition edited by Phillips Bradley.
7. *Ibid.*, I, 6.
8. *Ibid.*, ix.
9. Mill, "Tocqueville on Democracy," I, vi.
10. Lively, p. 33.
11. Gargan, "Tocqueville and the Problem of Historical Prognosis," p. 335; see also Marcel, pp. 86–87; Aron, p. 202; Faguet, pp. 79–80.
12. Tocqueville, *Democracy*, I, 3.
13. *Ibid.*, p. 6.
14. *Ibid.*, pp. 6–7.
15. *Ibid.*, I, 7.
16. Lively, p. 33.
17. Tocqueville, *Democracy*, I, 433, 166, 390–91.
18. Tocqueville, *Memoir*, II, 105.
19. Tocqueville, *Recollections*, p. 81.
20. Tocqueville, *European Revolution*, pp. 228–29.
21. Tocqueville, *Recollections*, p. 64. The same sentiment is expressed in the *Democracy*, II, 90–93.

22. Tocqueville, *Democracy*, II, 352.

23. *Ibid.*, p. 92.

24. *Ibid.*

25. *Ibid.*, p. 93.

26. Tocqueville to Mill, Oct. 27, 1843, in Tocqueville, *Oeuvres Complètes* (Mayer), VI, Part 1, 345.

27. Mill, *System of Logic*, p. 549.

28. Tocqueville, *Democracy*, I, 7.

29. *Ibid.*, p. ix, italics mine.

30. Mill, "Tocqueville," p. xiii.

31. Tocqueville to Gobineau, Dec. 20, 1853, in *European Revolution*, p. 232.

32. Tocqueville to Corcelle, July 22, 1854, in *Memoir*, II, 260.

33. Tocqueville to Mrs. Grote, July 24, 1850, in *Memoir*, II, 105.

34. Tocqueville to Corcelle, Oct. 23, 1854, in *Memoir*, II, 271.

35. See below, pp. 116.

36. See, e.g., Lively, p. 199; below, pp. 118–21.

37. Tocqueville, *Democracy*, II, 44, italics mine.

38. Janet, p. 117.

39. *Ibid.*, p. 118.

40. Tocqueville, *Democracy*, II, 340.

41. *Ibid.*, I, 8–9.

42. *Ibid.*, p. 8.

43. *Ibid.*, p.. 223, italics mine.

44. *Ibid.*, pp. 223, 244.

45. *Ibid.*, II, 173; see also his graphic account of Mme. de Sévigné, 174–75.

46. *Ibid.*, I, 372.

47. *Ibid.*, p. 397.

48. *Ibid.*, p. 373.

49. *Ibid.*, pp. 438–39.

50. Tocqueville, *Memoir*, I, 247, translation amended.

51. Tocqueville, *European Revoultion*, p. 73.

52. Tocqueville, *Democracy*, I, 15, 17.

53. See, for example, his letter of Sept.5, 1843, in *European Revolution*, p. 193.

54. Tocqueville, *Democracy*, II, 244–45.

55. Tocqueville, *Old Régime*, pp. 30, 111.

56. *Ibid.*, p. 82.

57. Tocqueville, *Oeuvres Complètes* (Mayer), II, 147.

58. Tocqueville, *Democracy*, I, 54.
59. *Ibid.*, p. 248.
60. *Ibid.*, p. 250; see also his *Journey to England and Ireland*, p. 72; also the excellent account in Drescher, pp. 50–51, 121–22.
61. Tocqueville, *Democracy*, I, 197; also 221–22, 248–49.
62. *Ibid.*, p. 247.
63. *Ibid.*, p. 250.
64. *Ibid.*, p. 48.
65. Tocqueville, *Journey to England and Ireland*, p. 158.
66. Drescher, p. 122.
67. See Tocqueville, *Democracy*, I, 310.
68. *Ibid.*, II, 242–43, translation amended.
69. *Ibid.*, pp. 244, 247, 251, 248.
70. *Ibid.*, pp. 242–43 (translation amended), 248.
71. *Ibid.*, pp. 254–55, italics mine, translation amended.
72. Berns, p. 369.
73. Cited in Pierson, p. 454.

II

1. Tocqueville, *Democracy*, II, 351.
2. Tocqueville, *Memoir*, I, 19–20.
3. Tocqueville, *Old Régime*, p. xii.
4. Tocqueville, *Democracy*, I, 15.
5. *Ibid.*, p. 327.
6. *Ibid.*, II, 271–72.
7. *Ibid.*, I, 223.
8. *Ibid.*, p. 377.
9. *Ibid.*, II, pp. 16, 17; *Oeuvres Complètes* (Mayer), I, Part II, 22.
10. Tocqueville, *Oeuvres Complètes* (Beaumont), VIII, 448.
11. Tocqueville, *Democracy*, I, 26.
12. *Ibid.*, II, 246.
13. Tocqueville to Madame Swetchine, Oct. 15, 1855, *Memoir*, II, 299–300.
14. Tocqueville, *Democracy*, I, 337, italics mine.
15. *Ibid.*, p. 48.
16. *Ibid.*, II, 352.
17. *Ibid.*, p. 71.
18. Tocqueville, *European Revolution*, p. 102.
19. Bryce, *Predictions*, pp. 24–25; cf. Lively, pp. 26–27.

20. See, e.g., Tocqueville, *Democracy*, I, 330ff.

21. *Ibid.*, p. 343.

22. *Ibid.*, pp. 409–10, 443–44.

23. Lively, p. 27.

24. Tocqueville, *Memoir*, II, 35.

25. Aristotle, 1317^a40–1317^b17.

26. Montesquieu, Bks. XX, XXI; see also Lowenthal, "Montesquieu," pp. 473, 478–88.

27. Faguet, p. 81.

28. Tocqueville, *Journey to America*, p. 260.

29. Tocqueville, *Democracy*, II, 211; cf., however, I, 315.

30. *Ibid.*, II, 105.

31. *Ibid.*, p. 104.

32. *Ibid.*, p. 5.

33. *Ibid.*, p. 104.

34. *Ibid.*, pp. 12–13.

35. Rousseau, p. 237.

36. Tocqueville, *Democracy*, II, 27.

37. Tocqueville, *European Revolution*, p. 206.

38. Tocqueville, *Democracy*, II, 140f, translation amended; cf. *Old Régime*, p. 118; also *Recollections*, p. 3.

39. Tocqueville, *Democracy*, II, 140.

40. *Ibid.*, pp. 144–45.

41. *Ibid.*

42. *Ibid.*, p. 219; cf. pp. 164*n*, 165.

43. Tocqueville, *Recollections*, p. 3.

44. Tocqueville, *Democracy*, II, 173.

45. *Ibid.*, p. 82.

46. *Ibid.*, p. 176.

47. *Ibid.*, pp. 100–101.

48. *Ibid.*, pp. 101–2.

49. *Ibid.*, p. 102.

50. *Ibid.*, I, 56.

51. Cf. *ibid.*, I, 342, with II, 334ff.

52. *Ibid.*, II, 337.

53. *Ibid.*, p. 313.

54. Tocqueville, *Old Régime*, p. 163.

55. Tocqueville, *Democracy*, II, 335.

56. Mill, "Tocqueville on Democracy," p. xxxviii.

57. The literature is extensive. See, e.g., Dunning, pp. 277–78;

the essay by Phillips Bradley in Tocqueville, *Democracy*, II, 454;
and Dahl, *passim*. Dahl would not argue, I believe, that rule by minorities constitutes any special danger to democracy. For a useful discussion of the problem of majority tyranny, see Sartori, pp. 98–102.

58. On special interest groups, see *Democracy*, II, 171; on the
fluctuation of the majority, see I, 257, 266, 279; II, 266.

59. *Ibid.*, II, 271; cf. 272, 276, 277.

60. Dahl, p. 132.

61. Tocqueville, *Democracy*, I, 180.

62. *Ibid.*, I, 265.

63. *Ibid.*, p. 277. Cf. the description of the "fatalism of the multitude" with that of the "tyranny of the majority," in Bryce, *American
Commonwealth*, II, 341–58.

64. Tocqueville, *Democracy*, I, 221.

65. *Ibid.*, p. 222.

66. *Ibid.*, II, 266–67.

67. *Ibid.*, pp. 145–46.

68. See Goldstein, p. 41; Drescher, pp. 9–10; Salomon, "Tocqueville's Philosophy of Freedom," pp. 412–17.

69. Strauss, *Natural Right and History*, pp. 252ff.

70. Tocqueville, *Democracy*, I, 262.

71. *Ibid.*, II, 269, translation amended.

72. *Ibid.*, p. 277.

73. Laski, p. 114.

III

1. Jaffa, *Crisis*, p. 416*n1*.

2. Tocqueville, *Democracy*, II, 351–52.

3. *Ibid.*, p. 340.

4. *Ibid.*, p. 113.

5. Tocqueville, *Old Régime*, p. xiv; cf. p. 275*n50*.

6. Tocqueville, *Democracy*, II, 304–5.

7. *Ibid.*, pp. 311n, 313.

8. *Ibid.*, I, 336.

9. *Ibid.*, p. 172.

10. Kant, p. 33.

11. Tocqueville to Corcelle, Sept. 17, 1853, in Tocqueville, *Memoir*, II, 230; see also *Democracy*, I, 126–27.

12. Rousseau, pp. 38–39.

13. Tocqueville, *Democracy*, I, 97, 118, 143.

14. *Ibid.*, II, 111, translation amended.

15. *Ibid.*, I, 98.

16. *Ibid.*, II, 112, 110.

17. *Ibid.*, I, 295.

18. *Ibid.*, II, 124–25. Cf. Tocqueville's analysis of associations with the opinions of Rousseau, *Social Contract*, Bk. II, chap. 3, 23–24, and *Discourse on Political Economy*, pp. 237–38.

19. Tocqueville, *Memoir*, I, 250.

20. George, pp. 12, 14, 17.

21. Tocqueville, *Democracy*, II, 115–16.

22. *Ibid.*, pp. 127–28.

23. *Ibid.*, p. 127.

24. *Ibid.*, italics mine. Cf. the discussion of the role of commercial interests in Diamond, pp. 64–67.

25. Lipset, p. 27.

26. *Ibid.*, p. 26.

27. Faguet, p. 101.

28. Tocqueville, *Democracy*, I, 62, 291.

29. *Ibid.*, p. 63.

30. *Ibid.*, II, 313.

31. *Ibid.*, II, 387.

32. Leroy, p. 484.

33. Tocqueville, *Democracy*, I, 11.

34. *Ibid.*, II, 131, translation amended.

35. *Ibid.*, I, 197.

36. *Ibid.*, p. 255, translation amended.

37. *Ibid.*

38. For a brief historical sketch of the problem, see Fromm, "Selfishness, Self-Love, and Self-Interest," pp. 401–20.

39. Tocqueville, *Democracy*, II, 131–32.

40. *Ibid.*, p. 129.

41. *Ibid.*, p. 131.

42. Cf. Tocqueville, *Old Régime*, pp. 118–19.

43. Tocqueville, *Democracy*, II, 132.

44. *Ibid.*, I, 252.

45. Rousseau, p. 3.

46. See also Rousseau, p. 275.

47. Tocqueville, *Oeuvres Complètes* (Mayer), V, Part 1, 235.

48. Tocqueville, *Democracy*, I, 408.

49. Washington, XXX, 294; XXXV, 229.

50. Cf. Tocqueville, *Democracy*, I, 318.
51. Rousseau, p. 139.
52. Tocqueville, *Democracy*, II, 133, translation amended.
53. *Ibid.*, pp. 133f.
54. See below, pp. 145–46.
55. Tocqueville, *Democracy*, II, 9f.
56. *Ibid.*, p. 9.
57. *Ibid.*, p. 21.
58. Tocqueville, *Democracy*, II, 22.
59. *Ibid.*, p. 21.
60. Cited in Pierson, p. 287.
61. Tocqueville, *Democracy*, II, 21–22, translation amended.
62. *Ibid.*, I, 45.
63. *Ibid.*, p. 156; cf. Hobbes, p. 200.
64. Tocqueville, *Democracy*, II, 27.
65. *Ibid.*, p. 154.
66. *Ibid.*, p. 155, italics mine.
67. Leroy, p. 480; the quotation is from Eugène d'Eichthal, *Alexis de Tocqueville et la démocratie libérale* (Paris, 1897), p. 50.
68. Engels, pp. 237–38.
69. Miller, p. 4.
70. Tocqueville, *Democracy*, I, 24–26.
71. *Ibid.*, pp. 356–57.
72. *Ibid.*, p. 26.
73. *Ibid.*, II, 154.
74. *Ibid.*, p. 153.
75. See Drescher, pp. 125–51.
76. In addition to Drescher, see Lively, p. 119; Salomon, "Tocqueville 1959," p. 453; Schapiro, pp. 559–61.
77. Tocqueville, *Democracy*, II, 39.
78. Mill, p. vii.
79. Tocqueville, *Democracy*, I, 306–7; cf. II, 161, 248.
80. *Ibid.*, I, 332–34.
81. *Ibid.*, p. 168.
82. *Ibid.*, II, 248.
83. *Ibid.*, p. 40, translation amended.
84. *Ibid.*, p. 268.
85. *Ibid.*, p. 266; cf. Diamond, pp. 64–67.
86. *Ibid.*, I, 261–62. Cf. I, 95–96; II, 341.
87. Tocqueville, *Journey to England*, p. 116.

88. *Ibid.*; Drescher, p. 127.

89. Tocqueville, *Journey to England*, p. 116, italics mine.

90. See, e.g., Cropsey, especially chap. 2; also Tocqueville, *European Revolution*, p. 206.

91. Tocqueville, *Democracy*, I, 305, 446; II, 160, 249–50, 293.

92. Tocqueville, *Journey to England*, p. 115.

93. Tocqueville, *Democracy*, I, 7.

94. *Ibid.*, II, 203n1; cf. I, 48, 50.

95. Salomon, "Tocqueville, Moralist and Sociologist," p. 406.

96. Tocqueville, *Democracy*, II, 6.

97. *Ibid.*, italics mine.

98. *Ibid.*, I, 322.

99. Tocqueville, *Old Régime*, p. 140, translation amended.

100. Tocqueville, *Democracy*, I, 310; see p. 35 above.

101. Rousseau, *Social Contract*, Bk. 2, chap. 12, p. 53, translation amended; see also rest of chap. 12. Cf. Montesquieu, Bk. 19, especially chaps. 4, 14, 16.

102. Tocqueville, *Democracy*, I, 171, translation amended. On the role of mores and the legislator in modern political thought, see Strauss, *Natural Right and History*, pp. 286–90.

103. Tocqueville, *Democracy*, I, 8, translation amended.

104. *Ibid.*, p. 337, translation amended; see also p. 336.

105. Mayer, p. 90; *Oeuvres Complètes* (Beaumont), IX, 123.

106. Mayer, p. 88; *Oeuvres Complètes* (Beaumont), IX, 117.

IV

1. *Memoir*, I, 380–81.

2. Leroy, in Ebenstein, p. 475.

3. Tocqueville, *Democracy*, II, 148, 150–51.

4. Tocqueville, *Old Régime*, p. 168, translation amended, italics mine.

5. *Ibid.*

6. Tocqueville, *European Revolution*, p. 167.

7. *Ibid.*, pp. 167–68.

8. See pp. 93, 107 above.

9. "Tocqueville's Concept of Citizenship," p. 53.

10. Tocqueville, *European Revolution*, pp. 169–70, translation amended, italics mine.

11. See pp. 36–39 above.

12. Tocqueville, *Democracy*, II, 132.
13. *Ibid.*, I, 196–97.
14. Hofstadter, p. 16.
15. Faguet, p. 104.
16. Rousseau, p. 40.
17. Strauss, *Natural Right and History*, p. 287.

Bibliography

Aristotle. Politics.

Aron, Raymond. Les grandes doctrines de sociologie historique. Paris: Centre de Documentation Universitaire, 1961.

Berns, Laurence. "Thomas Hobbes," in History of Political Philosophy, Leo Strauss and Joseph Cropsey, eds. Chicago: Rand McNally, 1963.

Bradley, Phillips. "A Historical Essay," in Tocqueville, Democracy in America, Phillips Bradley, ed. New York: Vintage, 1960, II, 389–487.

Bryce, James. The American Commonwealth, ed. and abridged by Louis Hacker. New York: Capricorn, 1959, 2 vols.

———— The Predictions of Hamilton and de Tocqueville. Johns Hopkins University Studies in Historical and Political Science, Series 5, No. 9.

Cicero. Offices.

Cropsey, Joseph. Polity and Economy: An Interpretation of the Principles of Adam Smith. The Hague: Martinus Nijhoff, 1957.

Dahl, Robert A. A Preface to Democratic Theory. Chicago: Phoenix, 1963.

Diamond, Martin. "Democracy and the Federalist," *American Political Science Review*, LIII (1959), Mar.

Drescher, Seymour. Tocqueville and England. Cambridge, Mass.: Harvard University Press, 1964.

Dunning, William A. A History of Political Theories from Rousseau to Spencer. New York: Macmillan, 1920.

Engels, Friedrich. "Ludwig Feuerbach and the End of Classical German Philosophy," in Marx and Engels, Basic Writings on Politics and Philosophy, Lewis S. Feuer, ed. Garden City, N.Y.: Anchor, 1959.

Faguet, Emile. Politicians and Moralists of the Nineteenth Century. Boston: Little, Brown, n.d.

Fromm, Erich. Man for Himself. New York: Rinehart, 1947.

————— "Selfishness, Self-Love, and Self-Interest," in Essays in Philosophy, Houston Peterson, ed. New York: Pocket Books, 1959.

Fustel de Coulanges, Numa Denis. The Ancient City, Willard Small, trans. Garden City, N.Y.: Anchor, n.d.

Gargan, Edward T. De Tocqueville. New York: Hillary House, 1965.

————— "Tocqueville and the Problem of Historical Prognosis," *American Historical Review*, LXVIII, No. 2 (Jan. 1963).

————— "Reply to Wyndham Lewis," *Sewanee Review*, LV (1947), supp.

George, William Henry. "Montesquieu and de Tocqueville and Corporative Individualism," *American Political Science Review*, XVI (1922).

Goldstein, Doris S. "Alexis de Tocqueville's Concept of Citizenship," *Proceedings of the American Philosophical Society*, CVIII (1964), No. 2.

————— "The Religious Beliefs of Alexis de Tocqueville," *French Historical Studies*, I (1960), Dec.

Hamilton, Alexander. The Works of Alexander Hamilton, Henry Cabot Lodge, ed. New York: Putnam, 1904, 12 vols.

Herr, Richard. Tocqueville and the Old Regime. Princeton, N.J.: Princeton University Press, 1962.

Hobbes, Thomas. Leviathan. Oxford: Blackwell, n.d.

Hofstadter, Richard. The American Political Tradition. New York: Vintage, 1957.

Jaffa, Harry V. "The Case for a Stronger National Government," in A Nation of States, R. Goldwin, ed. Chicago: Rand McNally, 1961.

————— Crisis of the House Divided. Garden City, N.Y.: Doubleday, 1959.

Janet, Paul. "Alexis de Tocqueville et la science politique au XIX siècle," *Revue des Deux Mondes*, XXXIV (1861).

Jefferson, Thomas. The Writings of Thomas Jefferson, Albert E. Bergh, ed. Washington, D.C.: Thomas Jefferson Memorial Association, 1907, 20 vols.

Kant, Immanuel. Perpetual Peace. New York: Columbia University Press, 1939.

Keeney, James. "Tocqueville and the New Politics," *New Politics*, I (1962), No. 3.

Laboulaye, Edouard. "Alexis de Tocqueville," in L'état et ses limites. Paris: Charpentie, 1871.

Laski, Harold J. "Alexis de Tocqueville," in The Social and Political

Ideas of Some Representative Thinkers of the Victorian Age, F.J.C. Hearnshaw, ed. New York: Barnes & Noble, 1930.

Leroy, Maxime. "Alexis de Tocqueville," in William Ebenstein, Political Thought in Perspective. New York: McGraw-Hill, 1957.

Lewis, Wyndham. "De Tocqueville and Democracy," *Sewanee Review*, LIV (1946).

Lipset, Seymour Martin. Political Man: The Social Bases of Politics. Garden City, N.Y.: Doubleday, 1960.

Lively, Jack. The Social and Political Thought of Alexis de Tocqueville. Oxford: Clarendon Press, 1962.

Locke, John. Two Treatises of Government. New York: Hafner, 1947.

Lowenthal, David. "Van Alstyne on the Establishment of Religion: An Alternative View," *American Political Science Review*, LIII (1964), June.

———— "Montesquieu," in History of Political Philosophy, Leo Strauss and Joseph Cropsey, eds. Chicago: Rand McNally, 1963.

Marcel, R. P. Essai politique sur Alexis de Tocqueville. Paris: Alcan, 1940.

Mayer, J. P. Alexis de Tocqueville: A Biographical Study in Political Science. New York: Harper Torchbooks, 1960.

Meyers, Marvin. The Jacksonian Persuasion: Politics and Belief. Stanford, Calif.: Stanford University Press, 1957.

Mill, John Stuart. Autobiography. London: Oxford University Press, 1949.

———— "De Tocqueville on Democracy in America," in Tocqueville, Democracy in America. New York: Schocken, 1961, 2 vols.

———— System of Logic. London: Longmans, Green, 1919.

Miller, William Lee, et al. Religion and the Free Society. New York: Fund for the Republic, 1958.

Montesquieu, Baron de. The Spirit of the Laws, Thomas Nugent, trans. New York: Hafner, 1959.

Nef, John. "Truth, Belief, and Civilization: Tocqueville and Gobineau," *Review of Politics*, XXV (1963), No. 4 (Oct.).

Pierson, George W. Tocqueville in America, abridged by Dudley C. Lunt. Garden City, N.Y.: Anchor, 1959.

Plato. Phaedo.

———— Republic.

Redier, Antoine. Comme disait M. de Tocqueville. Paris: Perrin, 1925.

Resh, Richard. "Alexis de Tocqueville and the Negro: *Democracy in America* Reconsidered," *Journal of Negro History*, XLVIII (1963), No. 4.

Richter, Melvin. "Tocqueville on Algeria," *Review of Politics*, XXV (1963), No. 3 (July).

Rousseau, Jean-Jacques. The Social Contract and Discourses. New York: Dutton, 1950.

Salomon, Albert. "Tocqueville, Moralist and Sociologist," *Social Research*, II (1935), No. 4.

———— "Tocqueville, 1959," *Social Research*, XXVI (1959), No. 4.

———— "Tocqueville's Philosophy of Freedom: A Trend Toward Concrete Sociology," *Review of Politics*, I (1939), No. 4.

Sartori, Giovanni. Democratic Theory. Detroit: Wayne State University Press, 1962.

Schapiro, J. S. "Alexis de Tocqueville, Pioneer of Democratic Liberalism in France," *Political Science Quarterly*, LVII (1942).

Schumpeter, Joseph A. Capitalism, Socialism and Democracy. New York: Harper Torchbooks, 1962.

Smith, Adam. Adam Smith's Moral and Political Philosophy, H. W. Schneider, ed. New York: Hafner, 1948.

Strauss, Leo. "The Liberalism of Classical Political Philosophy," *Review of Metaphysics*, XII (1958–59).

———— Natural Right and History. Chicago: University of Chicago Press, 1953.

———— and Joseph Cropsey, eds. History of Political Philosophy. Chicago: Rand McNally, 1963.

Tocqueville, Alexis de. Democracy in America, Phillips Bradley, ed. New York: Vintage, 1958, 2 vols.

———— The European Revolution and Correspondence with Gobineau, John Lukacs, ed. & trans. Garden City, N.Y.: Anchor, 1959.

———— Journey to America, J. P. Mayer, ed. New Haven, Conn.: Yale University Press, 1960.

———— Journey to England and Ireland, J. P. Mayer, ed. New Haven, Conn.: Yale University Press, 1958.

———— Memoir, Letters, and Remains of Alexis de Tocqueville. Boston, Mass.: Ticknor and Fields, 1862, 2 vols.

———— Oeuvres Complètes, J. P. Mayer, ed. Paris: Gallimard, 1951, 13 vols.

———— Oeuvres Complètes, pub. par Mme. de Tocqueville; Beaumont, ed. Paris: Michel Levy, 1864–67, 9 vols.

———— The Old Régime and the French Revolution, Stuart Gilbert, trans. Garden City, N.Y.: Anchor, 1955.

———— The Recollections of Alexis de Tocqueville, Alexander de Mattos, trans. New York: Meridian, 1959.

Wach, Joachim. "The Role of Religion in the Social Philosophy of Alexis de Tocqueville," *Journal of the History of Ideas*, VII (1946), Jan.

Washington, George. The Writings of George Washington, John C. Fitzpatrick, ed. Washington: Government Printing Office, 1939, 39 vols.

Index

Index